D0283802

MYRTLEFIELD
HOUSE

The Definition of Christianity

Myrtlefield Encounters

Myrtlefield Encounters are complementary studies of biblical literature, Christian teaching and apologetics. The books in this series engage the minds of believers and sceptics. They show how God has spoken in the Bible to address the realities of life and its questions, problems, beauty and potential.

The Definition of Christianity

David Gooding

John Lennox

Myrtlefield Encounters

David Gooding and John Lennox have asserted their rights under the Copyright, Designs and Patents Act, 1988, to be identified as Authors of this work

© Myrtlefield Trust, 1992, 1997, 2014

All rights reserved. No part of this publication may be reproduced, stored in a retrieval system, or transmitted, in any form or by any means, electronic, mechanical, photocopying, recording or otherwise, without the prior permission of the publisher or a license permitting restricted copying. In the UK such licenses are issued by the Copyright Licensing Agency, 90 Tottenham Court Road, London W1P 9HE

All Scripture quotations, unless otherwise indicated, are taken from The Holy Bible, English Standard Version, copyright © 2001 by Crossway Bibles, a division of Good News Publishers. Used by permission

Cover design: Ben Bredeweg

Cover photo: © Gilbert Lennox. ‹http://gilbertlennoxphotography.com› Used by permission

First published 1992. Originally published as a series of articles in the Russian literary newspaper, *Literaturnaya Gazeta*

Published by The Myrtlefield Trust, 180 Mountsandel Road, Coleraine, N Ireland, BT52 1TB
w: www.myrtlefieldhouse.com
e: info@myrtlefieldhouse.com

ISBN: 978-1-874584-49-0 (pbk.)
ISBN: 978-1-874584-50-6 (PDF)
ISBN: 978-1-874584-51-3 (Kindle)
ISBN: 978-1-874584-52-0 (EPUB without DRM)

18 17 16 15   10 9 8 7 6 5

Contents

CHAPTER 1

The True Revolution

The famous Indian philosopher and statesman, Mahatma Gandhi, was once asked why he did not join the Christian church. He replied: 'Which one?' Undeniably, from a world-wide point of view, modern Christendom presents a very confused and confusing picture.

That has come about for a number of reasons: first, in the course of history many superstitious additions have collected about Christianity like barnacles on the hull of a ship—so many at times that they have threatened to sink the whole thing beneath the contempt of thoughtful people.

The other reason is a more serious one—after all, a discriminating observer can easily distinguish a ship from a barnacle! It is far more difficult for the outsider to distinguish original, historic Christianity from the diverse developments in doctrine and practice that have taken place within Christendom over the centuries. That is a tremendous pity, for they often obscure the basic original and unchangeable historical facts that constitute the permanent heart and essence of Christianity.

After all, Christianity is not essentially a system of morality (as is Confucianism) that has to be adapted to the changing fashion of the centuries or else become outmoded. Nor is it a system of abstract universal philosophical truths, the validity of which is independent of the thinkers who first perceived them. Nor is it like many a pagan religion was, a system of rituals which depended for their effectiveness on being performed correctly.

As Paul, spokesman for the early church, would put it, Christianity is good news concerning a historical person, Jesus Christ of Nazareth, who, on the human side was born of the royal seed of David, and demonstrated to be the Son of God with power by his resurrection from the dead (Rom 1:1-4). Jesus Christ is himself that good news: his person, his life—what he did, taught and claimed; his death—what it accomplished; and his resurrection, that demonstrated that his claims were true. These historic facts are the heart of the Christian gospel, and the New Testament is the record of them and their implications.

Of all the writers in the New Testament, the greatest literary and historical genius is undoubtedly Luke, the author of the Gospel that bears his name, and of its companion volume, the Acts of the Apostles. Ernest Renan, who had little enough sympathy with the contents of Luke's Gospel, described it as 'the most beautiful book in the world';[1] and Acts, though not in that same sense beautiful, serves a unique purpose, not only within the New Testament, but also in the corpus of world history.

In the New Testament we find that three other

1. *Les Évangiles et la seconde génération chrétienne* (Paris: Calmann Lévy, 1877), 283.

2

writers along with Luke tell us of the life, death, and resurrection of Christ. The bulk of the rest of the New Testament is composed of letters written to various groups of Christians. From this we gather that, by the time of writing, multiracial Christian churches had already been established with remarkable rapidity, not only in Palestine, where Christ had lived, but all over the Mediterranean world: in learned Athens; in brilliant but vicious commercial Corinth; in elegant Ephesus; in primitive Paphlagonia; and even in the metropolis of the empire, Rome itself.

The question immediately arises: how did it all get started? How did these churches come to be? Luke sets himself to answer that question. He is the one who tells us how Christian apostles and missionaries went throughout the Roman world and preached the gospel, and multitudes both of Jews and Gentiles, hearing the gospel, believed, found salvation through Christ and constituted themselves into Christian churches.

But deeper questions suggest themselves: what were the contents of this gospel? Obviously the early Christians did not wait to have their message defined by the stately creeds of later centuries before they could preach it. Nor did people have to wait for later doctrinal developments before they could believe and find salvation through Jesus Christ. What, then, was the message that proved so effective in the early years of Christianity? What were its essential features? Who defined them, and how did they come to be defined? It is this last question above all that Luke the historian sets himself to answer.

Before observing how he does it, we should notice how well qualified he was for such a task. First of all, he was a travelling companion of the apostle Paul, and witnessed first-hand the formation of many Christian churches and the preaching by which they were formed.

Secondly, during the two years when Paul was imprisoned at Caesarea, Luke was able to use the opportunity to consult the contemporaries of Jesus Christ and learn the basic facts from eye-witnesses of our Lord's ministry (so he tells us in the preface to his Gospel). It is true that Luke's work has been fiercely criticized, but modern research has demonstrated that where he can be tested he proves to be a reliable and accurate historian, as we see from the massively detailed and documented work by Colin Hemer, *The Book of Acts in the Setting of Hellenistic History*.[2]

However, the genius of Luke as a historian is seen above all in the fact that he has not attempted to chronicle every last detail of every journey made,[3] and every sermon preached by every single one of the Christian missionaries. Naturally, he was interested in the geographical spread of Christianity; witness the summaries with which he concludes each major section of his work, which, like the pealing of bells, proclaim the irresistible spread of the Word of God and the consequent multiplication of Christian churches. But when we examine his selection of material in each of those major sections, we can immediately see that his prime interest lay elsewhere.

Take, for instance the first section (Acts 1:1–6:7). Here Luke describes how the apostles, empowered by the Holy

2. Volume 49 of *Wissenschaftliche Untersuchungen zum Neuen Testament* (Tübingen: Mohr Siebeck, 1989).
3. For a fuller treatment of the validity of Luke's selective treatment of history, see *True to the Faith*, by David Gooding (Coleraine: Myrtlefield House, 2013), 503–13.

Spirit, were busy proclaiming the incontrovertible fact of the resurrection of Jesus, and pressing home upon their hearers its inescapable implication: God has made this Jesus, whom you crucified, both Lord and Christ, and salvation and forgiveness of sins are to be found in him and in him only. But then a crisis occurred—the Sanhedrin banned all preaching in the name of Jesus.

Now the Sanhedrin was for normative Judaism the supreme religious authority; the apostles had been brought up in Judaism, and Christianity had been born in its midst. To disobey and defy the Sanhedrin was a serious step to take and one fraught with all kinds of foreseeable and unforeseeable consequences.

But to obey the Sanhedrin was impossible without denying the very heart, life and soul of Christianity. To deny or keep silent about the deity and messiahship of the living Lord would have been disobedience to God, disloyalty to Christ and to the cause of man's salvation. Compromise was impossible. Without hesitation, the apostles disobeyed and defied the Sanhedrin; and Christianity took its first step away from official Judaism.

Thus, with a historian's fine sense of what was truly significant and important, Luke shows us the apostles of our Lord Jesus defining for all time what is the first major indispensable foundation of the Christian gospel.

In the second major section of the work (Acts 6:8–9:31) Stephen, the first Christian martyr, though he had been brought up to revere the Jewish temple, began to perceive that Christ's sacrifice on the cross, his resurrection and entry into heaven, carried implications that would eventually make that temple obsolete, along with its whole elaborate system of sacrifices, rituals, and priesthood. For advancing this view and maintaining it in public discussion, he was put on trial for his life. But he made no attempt to recant. For him, the Christian understanding of man's new way of approach to God, inaugurated by Christ, was so essential to the gospel that compromise was impossible. So Stephen died, and Christianity defined another element in its essential message.

In the third section (Acts 9:32–12:24), Luke tells how the ancient Jewish concept of holiness threatened to prevent the Christian message from leaping over the boundaries of Judaism into the vastly bigger Gentile world. God therefore had to intervene, to teach the apostle Peter how different Christianity was going to be from the Judaism in which he had been brought up. External ritualistic and ceremonial holiness, based on strict observance of dietary laws and religious washings, valid as it was in Old Testament days, was no longer appropriate.

In fact, it was now to be set aside. From this time on, holiness was to be achieved by a deep, inner, personal relationship with the living Lord. Cleansing from the guilt of sin was to be conveyed by the blood of his substitutionary sacrifice, and power to live a clean life was to be supplied by the indwelling Holy Spirit whom Christ imparts to all who personally put their trust in him.

The same pattern repeats itself in the fourth section (12:25–16:5). In Judaism, in which the early Christians had been reared, the initiatory rite of circumcision, normally performed on babies a few days after birth, was regarded as indispensable for membership in the holy nation; and helpful, if not necessary, for salvation. Some Christians began by thinking that this rite was still necessary for salvation; but at a meeting of the apostles and elders called in Jerusalem to consider the matter, Peter and James pronounced the official, authoritative and permanent apostolic decision. The religious rite of circumcision was unnecessary for and contributed absolutely nothing to salvation, not only in the case of the Gentiles but for Jews as well. It would be impossible to exaggerate the importance of the epoch-making step which Christianity took away from the ritualism of Judaism at that time.

Similarly in section five (16:6–19:20), when Paul and his companions eventually reached Macedonia and Greece, Luke, by a judicious selection of incidents and speeches, once more shows us Christianity defining itself against the background, not now of Judaism, but of pagan spiritism, politics, religion, and philosophy.

Finally, in the last and longest section of the book (19:21–28:31), the atmosphere of Luke's record is noticeably different, for Paul is to be found here not so much preaching but defending the gospel in the civil and religious courts of the empire. But the pattern is the same. For as Paul defends both himself and the gospel from the slanderous allegations that have been made against them, Luke's record makes clear that Paul and the gospel are not what people have ignorantly imagined them to be, or what people have maliciously represented them as being. Luke is thus continuing to define by contrast what Christianity really is.

Luke's fine sense of what was essential Christianity can be very enlightening for us who live in this distant century. For, in the ensuing ages, Christendom has often allowed its message to become confused with civil politics and contemporary philosophies. In fact, in some countries, pagan customs have been baptized into the church; and in our own day, obsession with the occult and fascination with various practices of Hinduism threaten to invade the church and lead to unholy syncretism. In wealthier countries temptation has been strong to join secret business associations which in their ceremonies worship the same old pagan deities as the ancient world did; while in poorer countries in recent decades there has been the opposite temptation to wed the Christian gospel with Marxism, to produce a politicized liberation theology.

Now Luke originally dedicated his work to a certain Theophilus in the hope of convincing him of the true nature and credibility of the Christian faith (Acts 1:1). As we study the detail of Luke's record, and Christianity stands forth in all its pristine clarity, it would be Luke's hope that he could do the same for us as he did for Theophilus.

CHAPTER 2

The Prime Definition

Ask what power it was that catapulted the early Christians on to the stage of world history, and Luke will unhesitatingly reply: the resurrection of Jesus, and the coming of the Holy Spirit. Ask again for what purpose the early Christian community came into existence, and Luke will once more reply: to witness to the resurrection of Jesus. Luke everywhere insists on this basic historical fact. This was the task, he tells us in his very first chapter, to which the risen Lord appointed his disciples (Acts 1:8). This was the purpose for the election of Matthias: to 'become with us a witness to his [Christ's] resurrection' (1:22). Thereafter, time and time again, he repeats that the prime function of the Christian community was to witness to the resurrection of the Lord Jesus.[1]

This is both remarkable and significant. Ask Buddhists, for instance, what the source of their religion is, and they will say: 'Gautama Buddha and his Enlightenment'. But at

1. See Acts 2:32; 3:15; 5:30–32; 10:39–41; 13:31; 17:3, 31; 26:16.

the time of his death, the Buddha denied that he himself was the means of salvation. It was his teaching that was all important. And the purpose of his followers has always been to practise and propagate that teaching.

The early Christians, by contrast, give a very different account of themselves. When Jesus died, they still possessed his wonderful ethical teachings. But, in spite of that, they felt that Jesus himself was a failure. He was not the deliverer that they thought he was going to be (Luke 24:19-21); and they cowered together in a bolted upper room for fear that they too might be arrested and executed.

What transformed them? Not a new insight into the value of Christ's ethical teachings. It was his resurrection that did it! And when they confronted the public, it was not primarily Christ's ethical teaching that they preached—there is scarcely one sentence from the Sermon on the Mount in the whole of Acts—it was the resurrection of Christ and all its glorious implications.

Now the Christian Church is a fact of history; and, from an historical point of view, its origin has to be accounted for. Obviously it did not arise causeless and purposeless out of nothing. If we refuse to believe in the resurrection, and therefore reject the only cause and purpose that the early Christians themselves give for their own origin and existence, it leaves a gaping hole in history that no other suggested cause can convincingly fill. Without the resurrection, the Christians would have lacked the courage to confront the world; and, on their own confession (1 Cor 15:1-20), they would have had no gospel to confront the world with.

As it is, what they preached was the good news about Jesus of Nazareth: 'that Christ died for our sins in accordance with the Scriptures, that he was buried, that he was raised on the third day in accordance with the Scriptures' (1 Cor 15:3-4). Now the resurrection of just any man at all, no matter who he was, would certainly be a startling piece of news; but it would not necessarily be gospel for the whole of mankind! The resurrection of Jesus is both credible and gospel for the whole world, because he—though certainly human like the rest of us—was not just any man at all: he was the climax of the age-long process of God's self-revelation to mankind.

In his first major sermon (Acts 2:25-31), the apostle Peter identifies him as the descendant of Israel's ancestral king David, and, in his second (3:12-26), as a physical and spiritual heir of Israel's patriarchs, Abraham, Isaac, and Jacob.

Before we dismiss these identifications as irrelevant for the purpose of defining a universal gospel, we should notice the prominence with which other New Testament writers advertise these facts. Matthew informs his largely Jewish readers that Jesus Christ was the Son of David, the Son of Abraham (Matt 1:1). More remarkable still, Paul, in his masterly explanation of the gospel written to the Christians in Rome, capital of the imperial Caesars, insists on identifying the gospel as good news 'concerning [God's] Son, who was descended from David according to the flesh' (Rom 1:1-3).

What apparent incongruity is this? The Roman Empire was still young when Jesus was born. After the convulsions of the civil war that brought the Roman Republic to its end, Augustus had managed to establish an empire that had largely pacified the world and was destined to last for a thousand years and more. It must have seemed ridiculous, if not offensive, to be told that not the Roman emperors but Jesus of Nazareth from the apparently defunct royal house of a tiny and sometimes troublesome nation on the edge of the empire, was God's appointed Saviour of the world!

Nonetheless, the early Roman governors and emperors were nobly tolerant of Christianity, as Luke himself in all fairness points out, even if sometimes they mocked Christians, as Festus mocked Paul, claiming they were mentally disturbed religious fanatics. As Christianity spread, however, later emperors—imagining that it was subversive of the State and contrary to its ideologies—tried to suppress it, making persistence in Christianity a capital offence against the State. The more brutal of them fed Christians to the lions.

And yet history has taught us its undeniable lessons. The great Caesars and their mighty empire have long since disappeared. None follows them now, none obeys them. Yet Christianity has proved irrepressible, underlining the truth of the advice that Gamaliel gave to his fellow counsellors on the Jewish Sanhedrin, during their first attempt to suppress Christianity:

> Keep away from these men and let them alone, for if this plan or this undertaking is of man, it will fail; but if it is of God, you will not be able to overthrow them. (Acts 5:38-39)

To this day, regimes which have neglected this advice, and have tried to suppress Christianity, have one by one either disappeared or have had to be dismantled. Yet increasing millions gladly bear allegiance to Jesus as the living Lord.

But there was another scandal attached to the Christian gospel which only the resurrection could overcome. Christ, while he lived, certainly claimed to be the Messiah, the Son of David. At the same time, he forewarned his disciples that he would not immediately ascend to his triumphal throne. He must first die and rise again. They found it incomprehensible. For they, like us, found it difficult to take in what they did not want to hear. Their concept of a Saviour was modelled on an inadequate understanding of King David, more in line with the comparatively recent exploits of the Maccabean freedom fighters. They looked for a Messianic king who would expel the hated imperialist forces of occupation, champion the poor, and eliminate the quislings who had exploited the Roman tax system for their own gain.

So, a Messiah who, instead of conquering his enemies, allowed himself apparently to be defeated by a corrupt and evil political system, was a contradiction in terms. When Jesus was arrested, they forsook him and fled, and when he was crucified their hopes were shattered (Luke 24:20-21). But the resurrection of Christ not only restored their faith in him: it infinitely enlarged their concept of salvation. Up to that point their analysis of the human problem had been far too shallow.

In the first place, it had been limited to their own narrow Jewish nationalistic interests; whereas Jesus was to be a deliverer for all mankind from whatever nation. Secondly, they had overlooked the fact that political activism and human warfare are very blunt instruments for putting right the injustices of the world. Great revolutionary movements have rarely managed to eliminate only the evil and leave the innocent unscathed: usually it has been the reverse. Moreover, professed campaigners for justice have sometimes eliminated millions on the basis of ideologies whose inevitable demise has betrayed the horrific cost in human lives at which their empires were built. If justice is ever to be done to these innumerable millions who have died, then death itself must be overcome.

The resurrection is God's triumphant proclamation that death is not the end, that the injustices of the past are not forgotten, that evil will not for ever triumph. As Peter points out to the crowd (Acts 2:33–36), King David himself had foreseen the necessity of this: if Messiah, like all other men, were to be abandoned permanently to the grave, then there was no ultimate end to the injustices of earth except one eternal, indiscriminate, appallingly unjust grave. In raising Jesus Christ from the dead, God has given advance notice and assurance to all men that death is not the end, that injustices will not for ever triumph. God will one day judge the world in righteousness by that same Jesus Christ (17:31).

Peter, in fact, began his sermon by pointing out that the prophet Joel, along with all the other prophets, had fortified his hearers with the promise of that day of universal judgment: the 'great and glorious Day of the Lord', he called it (2:20). The resurrection of Jesus Christ confirmed that promise, and Peter preached it as gospel to the nation.

There is, of course, an understandable objection to this claim, and it goes like this: If all this is true, why has it not happened yet? Why has evil been allowed to run unchecked so long and to rise to such monstrous proportions in our own century? The answer once more is to be found in what Peter pointed out to the crowd. The programme that God originally gave through David, the ancient king and prophet, had never been that the Messiah, after his death and resurrection, would proceed immediately to put down evil by force throughout the whole world. He would ascend to God's heavenly throne, and be there until, at his second coming, all his enemies would be put under his feet (Ps 110:1-2; Acts 2:34-35).

And we ourselves can see why this had to be so. The promise of a coming judgment is not unqualified good news for us all. For while we have all been sinned against, we have all personally sinned, and that not only against other people but against God. And if no remedy can be found for this, then the coming judgment would spell disaster for us and for the whole human race.

It is this that gives universal significance to Luke's next identification of the gospel. Isaiah the prophet had long since indicated that the Messiah had another God-given role to fulfil. Before he came as king to judge the world, he was to come as God's Servant who would not only suffer innocently at man's hands, without retaliation—that would have left evil forever triumphant, and would have saved nobody—but who would take on himself the penalty of the sins of the world, suffer and die as a sacrifice for sin, so that men and women might be forgiven, justified, and accepted with God (Isa 52:13-53:12).

It was to this that Jesus himself referred, when he remarked to his apostles: 'The Son of Man came not to be served, but to serve and to give his life a ransom for many'

(Matt 20:28). It was to this that Peter referred when, to the very men who had shouted for Christ's crucifixion, he preached Jesus as God's perfect servant through whom they might find forgiveness, peace, and reconciliation with God.[2]

But how were Peter's hearers to know that it was all true? They had not seen the risen Lord, as the apostles had. They could, of course, have gone to the tomb and found it empty. They could have investigated all the other evidence, both material and human. But, on top of that, there was evidence of another kind.

Luke tells us that it was nothing less than this: the resurrection and ascension of Jesus Christ had opened the way for that unprecedented invasion of the Holy Spirit of God into our world, that Joel the ancient prophet had predicted 800 years before. The evidence for it was at two levels. At one level, it was already assailing the ears of the polyglot crowd, drawn from all over the world to Jerusalem on the occasion of the Jewish Feast of Pentecost. For the Holy Spirit on that occasion had empowered the early Christians miraculously to speak in foreign languages which they had not learned, and did not understand, in such a way that those in the crowd who were native speakers of those languages could understand what was being said. The point and the purpose of that unusual miracle was clearly to demonstrate that both the message which the apostles preached, and the convicting power by which they spoke, came from God himself.

At another level, the effectiveness of the evidence depended on their willingness to conduct a personal

---

2. Acts 3:13—the Greek should be translated 'servant', and not 'son'.

experiment. They were, as Peter pointed out, being offered the gift of the Holy Spirit (Acts 2:38). The reception of him into their hearts would open up vigorous personal fellowship with God, that would provide incontrovertible evidence that Jesus, the Son of David, the Son of Abraham, was indeed the Saviour for the world. For this there were terms and conditions of course; and of that we shall speak in our next chapter.

CHAPTER 3

The World's Fatal Flaw

It is the opinion of many that the chief business of Christianity—if it has any true business at all—should be to concern itself with moral issues and human values: to denounce lying, theft, and adultery, and all such individual sins, and at the same time to encourage people to forgive their enemies, to love and be kind to one another. If that is our impression, we are in for a shock when we first open the pages of Luke's history and read for ourselves his record of the very first sermons which the Christians preached. They do not concern themselves with denouncing individual sins, nor with encouraging people to develop worthy virtues. That is not because the early Christians were indifferent to ethical issues and human values: the letters which the apostles wrote to their early converts are full of such moral instruction.

Luke's record shows that the early Christians' apparent lack of interest in individual sins was because they were preoccupied with one particular sin of overwhelming significance. The resurrection of Christ had demonstrated him to be the Son of God with power; and the inevitable implication was appalling: Israel had crucified their God-sent Messiah; human beings had killed the source of their life (Acts 3:15); mankind had murdered its Maker. The crucifixion of Christ, as the early Christians saw it (basing themselves on the Bible), was sheer human rage against God: a concerted effort by both Jews and Gentiles to cast off God's restraint and claims on them (4:23-31).

This is no exaggeration. The cross of Christ diagnoses what the basic trouble of the whole world is at all times. It is not man's hostility to man: that is only a secondary symptom. It is man's hostility to God. The crucifixion of God's Son was but the cone of a volcano through which, at a certain time and place in history, there erupted that deep-lying resentment and rebellion against God which ever since man first sinned have smouldered in everybody's heart, religious or irreligious, ancient or modern.

The parable of the Vineyard Keepers (Luke 20:9-15), which our Lord told primarily against the religious leaders of his time, makes the same point. The world we live in has a personal owner, and it is not us! We are but tenants and stewards. And the heir to the vineyard is the owner's son.

But people are not content to be tenants. They live as if there were no landlord. Or if there is, they live as if he had no right to expect any dues of love, obedience, devotion, and service from them. They act as if they owned the complete freehold of their own lives, as if the world belonged to them. They have no love for the owner's son for whom in fact the universe was made, who was the agent in its creation, is the maintainer of its present stability, and is its redeemer and eventual restorer (Col 1:16–20; Heb 1:1–3).

As long as he keeps his distance, of course, the world doesn't mind him. They can even affect a certain amount of religion. But let him approach, insist on his ownership and demand his dues—then the resistance starts. They denounce his demands as absolutism. They fight for their independence. They may, like the pseudo-Christian apostle, Judas, talk much about their concern for the poor (John 12:4–6); but like Judas they will readily deny God and Christ in order to gain or keep a place for themselves in the world (Acts 1:15–20). But to sell one's Creator for thirty pieces of silver is to evince a value system that is fatally flawed. Sell your Creator for any sum, and you automatically reduce the value of your fellow-creatures catastrophically. And then, as a result, you must not be surprised to find yourself conniving at the elimination of thousands of human beings, if only social and political improvement seems to call for it.

As Dostoevsky says, 'Without God ... everything is permitted.'[1] Atheism's claim that you can eliminate all talk of God from morality, and base ethics simply on man's inherent value, is fraudulent. It is like eliminating a bank's reserves, and still expecting people to honour its bank notes. It will not cure man's chaotic value system; it is itself the cause of a tragic devaluation of man.

If this, then, is how the early Christians diagnosed mankind's basic sin, it is of more than historical interest

---

1. The statement is made by one of Fyodor Dostoevsky's characters in *The Brothers Karamozov*, tr. Richard Peavar and Larissa Volokhonsky (San Francisco: North Point Press, 1990).

to notice Luke's account of the astonishing offer of mercy, forgiveness, and reconciliation, which God authorized Peter to make to the very murderers of his Son. There was first of all the offer of 'the forgiveness of your sins' (Acts 2:38). Note the plural 'sins' and the personal adjective 'your' sins (2:38). Forgiveness not only of the particular sin of crucifying Christ, but of all sins—the wiping of the heart clean from the guilt of every transgression. And then, in addition, the offer of the gift of the Holy Spirit, who would establish a living and personal relationship between God and every believer, a sharing of the very life of God.

If this, then, was how Peter defined salvation, what terms and conditions did he lay down for receiving it? They were simplicity itself. The key demand was: Repent!

But then what was meant by repentance in this situation? First, we should notice the flow of thought that runs from the end of Joel's prophecy, which Peter quoted at the beginning of his sermon (2:17-21), to the climax with which he concluded it (2:36). Joel had warned that there was coming a day when his hearers must face the wrath of God on account of their sins. If they would be saved from that wrath, they must call on the name of the Lord.

For the crowd at Jerusalem, then, repentance would in the first place mean turning round and facing the fact that, in spite of all their previous religiosity, they needed to be saved from God's wrath.

Secondly, it would mean facing the (for them) alarming fact which the resurrection had demonstrated: God had made the very Jesus, whom they had crucified, both Lord and Christ (2:36). If now they wanted to be saved, mere promises of better behaviour in the future would scarcely suffice. They must swallow their pride, turn about face, call on the very Jesus whom they had crucified, acknowledge him as Lord, and cry for his mercy. He it was who would personally give them the Holy Spirit, and establish their relationship with God.

Thirdly, while they had the Bible's own explicit assurance that if in genuine repentance they called on the name of the Lord Jesus, they would most certainly be saved, they were required to demonstrate that their repentance was genuine. 'Calling on the name of the Lord' would have to be more than simply reciting a religious formula. It would mean capitulating to Jesus entirely, and accepting him as Lord of all they were and had. It would also mean publicly confessing him as Lord, not just in word, but in action. 'Repent', said Peter, 'and be baptized every one of you in the name of Jesus Christ' (2:38).

Of course, we must be careful not to read back into Christian baptism in these early times, the meanings that developed in later centuries. There is no evidence in Acts that baptism was regarded by the first Christians as a ritual which conveyed the gift of the Holy Spirit. In fact, the historical evidence goes quite the other way. Cornelius and his friends, whom Luke later presents as the archetypal example of Gentile conversion, received the Holy Spirit before they were baptized (10:47). Obviously, then, it was not dependent on baptism. As Peter later explained, these Gentiles listened to him preaching that everyone who believes shall receive forgiveness of sins. They believed; and God, who read their hearts, gave public testimony to the fact that they had truly repented, and that their faith was genuine. He gave them the Holy Spirit there and then, having cleansed their hearts solely by faith. Only afterwards were they baptized, and then only on the ground that they had already received the Holy Spirit (10:44–48; 11:15–17; 15:7–9).

On the other hand, the mere consternation of the Jerusalem crowd and their anxiety over their crucifixion of Jesus did not in themselves amount to genuine repentance. A few weeks earlier, they had publicly denied before Pilate that Jesus was the Christ (3:13–14). If they did now genuinely repent, they must show it. They must reverse their previous verdict; they must confess that Jesus was the Christ, and do so just as publicly as they had earlier denied it, by being baptized 'in the name of Jesus Christ'. They had publicly stood with the murderers of Jesus, and shouted with them for his crucifixion. Now they must 'save [themselves] from this crooked generation' (2:40). They could not continue to stand with the murderers and still pretend to have repented of the murder. They must change sides; and baptism in the name of Jesus was a way of showing they had. If they were not prepared to do that, how would they convince anybody, let alone God, that their professed repentance was real?

Moreover, their repentance and their baptism in the name of Jesus Christ were not one-off events that had no further effect on their subsequent lifestyle. Luke tells us that thereafter they devoted themselves to 'the apostles' teaching and the fellowship, to the breaking of bread, and the prayers' (2:42); it was the natural outcome of their genuine repentance. Since they now believed that God had made Jesus of Nazareth both Lord and Christ, they would be eager to know in ever greater detail what the Holy

Spirit would reveal to them through the apostles about Christ's relationship to God and to the universe.

And when it says that the early Christians devoted themselves to the apostles' fellowship, it does not, of course, mean that they simply began to socialize with the apostles. It meant the outworking of the common life they had individually received through the Holy Spirit, which bound them together with the apostles and their Lord.

They were devoted to the breaking of bread, says Luke (and we notice the simplicity of the description by which this custom was named at this early period, answering to the actual simplicity of the custom itself). Before he died, Christ had called on his people constantly to remember him by simply eating bread together as a symbol of his body, and by drinking wine as a symbol of his blood; not in order to gain forgiveness, but in memory of him by whose sacrificial death they had already been forgiven. Sheer gratitude, if nothing else, would have led them lovingly to do it.

Likewise they devoted themselves to prayer. Now that they were reconciled to God and in fellowship with the ascended Lord, prayer ceased to be a mere formal routine and became active participation with the ruler of the universe.

Moreover, Luke is at pains to record (2:42–47) that the gospel and its implications revolutionized not only their spiritual life but their attitude to secular things as well. It even transformed their attitude to private property. But more of that in our next chapter.

CHAPTER 4

A Clash of World Views

The rights and wrongs of private property have naturally attracted the attention of various political philosophers and politicians all down the centuries; but it is perhaps a surprise to find the prominence which Luke devotes to the topic in the first major section of Acts.

The spectacular explosion of spiritual energy initiated on the day of Pentecost and its ever-increasing impact would automatically have forced themselves on the choice of any historian of the birth of Christianity to be included in his account. But, with a fine sense of balance, Luke has deliberately chosen to place an almost equal emphasis on the early Christians' attitude to material things, and to the question of private property.

> All who believed were together and had all things in common. And they were selling their possessions and belongings and distributing the proceeds to all, as any had need. (Acts 2:44–45)

> Barnabas ... sold a field that belonged to him and brought the money and laid it at the apostles' feet. (4:36–37)

> The full number of those who believed were of one heart and soul, and no one said that any of the things that belonged to him was his own, but they had everything in common. (4:32)

And on top of all this, one of the miracles which Luke chooses to describe in detail during this period is the summary judgment inflicted on a certain Ananias and Sapphira, for what was seen as their deliberate collusion in an attempt to deceive both the apostles and God over the matter of their property (5:1–11).

What, then, shall we make of this phenomenon of the early Christian community of goods? The first thing to notice is that it was entirely voluntary. Peter explicitly told the aforesaid Ananias and Sapphira that their piece of land was their own private property. They were not forced by the Christian faith, nor by the church, nor, of course, by the State, to sell it and give the money to the church or to anyone else. And once they had sold the land, they still had the right to decide how to dispose of the money, if in fact they wanted to dispose of it. They did not have to pay it in to the central funds of the Christian group. Compulsory community of goods was no part of the Christian faith; history demonstrates what misery and disaster can result from that kind of pressure.

Secondly, we should not exaggerate or mistranslate what the Greek of 4:34 says. Not every property owner who got converted immediately sold all his lands and houses and gave the money away. What happened was that property owners would from time to time sell part of their holdings and use the money to meet particular needs which arose in the Christian community.

The important thing to grasp about the early Christian attitude to material possessions was the motivation which lay behind it. 'No one said,' says Luke, 'that any of the things that belonged to him was his own' (4:32). Whose then? we ask. And the answer is, Christ's. If they sold their possessions and laid the money at the apostles' feet, it was because the apostles were the official representatives of Christ. If they kept their possessions and did not sell or give them away, they would still have regarded them not as their own but as Christ's, and themselves simply as stewards responsible to administer them for the good of the community.

This still is, or ought to be, the true Christian's attitude to material possessions, for it springs from the realization that Jesus Christ is not merely a prophet or moral teacher: he is the Lord and owner of Creation. The believer, there-fore, is taught that if Christ gave his life's blood to redeem him from the ruinous consequences of his insane rebellion against his Creator, then the believer himself is no longer his own property. He has been bought with a price.[1] All that he is and has belongs to Christ, and is to be used in responsible stewardship in the interests of Christ, for the good of his people and of mankind in general, for the evan-gelization of the world, and for the furtherance of God's purposes in the earth.

1. 1 Cor 6:19–20; 2 Cor 5:14–15.

But the topic goes deeper. One cannot read this first section of Acts without perceiving that, unlike some eastern religions, Christianity does not regard the material world as an illusion from which the truly wise man tries to escape. Unlike Platonic philosophy, it does not regard the body as the tomb of the soul, and hold that the soul should attempt to keep aloof from the body as much as possible. Christianity certainly teaches that the body should be disciplined and kept in proper control (1 Cor 9:27); but it disapproves of systematic neglect of the body as a means to salvation and holiness (Col 2:16–23). Understandably so. For the cornerstone of the Christian gospel is the bodily resurrection of Christ. Luke pointedly refers in his introduction to Acts (1:3), to what he had recorded in greater detail at the end of his Gospel (Luke 24:36–43). The risen Lord was not a disembodied soul or spirit. He had a human body, glorified—but nonetheless real and tangible. For the human body is an integral part of the human personality. God created it so, and is not ashamed of it.

Moreover, the gospel, according to the first section of Acts, is that God is not concerned merely with the spiritual salvation of individuals. He has plans for the complete restoration of the physical creation. This, as Peter's second major sermon declares, has been the message of all God's prophets (Acts 3:21–26). The Bible knows nothing of Hinduism's degrading of the material universe into an endless, meaningless cycle of birth, death, and rebirth; nor anything of the modern atheist's pessimism in holding, as atheistic science forces him to, that all human life and progress will end in meaningless oblivion. The Bible affirms that the whole creation has a glorious destiny. The bodily resurrection of Jesus is the first fruits of the restoration of the entire universe; and the coming of the Holy Spirit to live in the bodies of believers is the first fruits of their great inheritance to come, when not only their physical bodies but creation itself will be delivered from its bondage to decay and brought into the glorious freedom of the children of God.[2]

Appropriately enough, then, the second major miracle in this section of Acts is the physical healing of a congenitally lame man (Acts 3). His physical handicap was a vivid example of the suffering of the whole creation; his miraculous healing a token in advance of its eventual restoration (3:21). Some will doubtless object: if there is a God, and he empowered Peter miraculously to heal this lame man, why did he not heal all sick people throughout the world? And why does he still delay to do so?

But there is a reason, as Peter explained to the crowd. They had murdered the very author of life (3:15). If they persisted in rejecting him, there could be nothing for them but eternal death. In his mercy, therefore, God was going to delay the time of the restoration of all things, that nature's very pains might lead, or even drive, them to repent (3:19), so that, reconciled to God, they might be ready to participate when God's plans for the redevelopment of the universe eventually swung into action.

The lesson is important for us, too. Our earth is not a self-created machine which just happens to have gone a little wrong, but which we with our increasing know-how and technology can put right, granted only sufficient

2. 1 Cor 15:20–25; Rom 8:18–25.

goodwill and international co-operation. Behind our earth stands a personal Creator and a personal Saviour. Not all the technological engineering, medical treatment, social aid, economic strategy, political prudence, and education of the masses that could ever be brought to bear upon earth's problems could finally solve them and produce a paradise, so long as the world remains at odds with its Creator, and rejects its appointed Saviour.

It was this kind of thing, then, that the Christian apostles were preaching when, according to Luke, the opposition erupted; and it came, not from atheists and humanists, but from the ruling party in Jerusalem, the Sadducees (4:1–22; 5:17–42). All of them were at least nominally religious: some of them were priests of the highest rank in the temple at Jerusalem. But they held a worldview that was diametrically opposed to that of the Christians.

As Luke elsewhere reminds us, the Sadducees did not believe in the possibility of resurrection, nor in the existence of angel or spirit (23:8). That, incidentally, gives the lie to the modern fallacy that the Christian gospel was invented in a pre-scientific age when people were all prepared to believe in miracles like resurrection because they did not know the laws of nature and science. The Sadducees were certainly not prepared to believe. And if Luke, the trained medical doctor, was, it was because he was convinced by an honest study of the evidence.

Now the Sadducees, Luke tells us (4:16), could not deny the evidence before their eyes of the miraculous healing of the lame man; but they were not prepared to allow it to upset their predetermined worldview. In this, of course, they were very much like us today. None of us comes to the study of cosmology or physics or biology with a completely open mind. We all have our pre-chosen worldviews, and it is they that determine our interpretation of the evidence, and not the other way round. What evidence fits into our worldview we accept; what does not, we tend to hold in abeyance.

Christians do it: for they frankly start from a God-based worldview. But the atheist does it as well. The Christian's worldview is based on faith produced and supported by an abundance of evidence. But the atheist's worldview is equally based on faith, for atheism cannot be proven. The question is: on which side lies the greater evidence? To ignore the evidence for Christianity is not scientific but obscurantism.

But to get back to the Sadducees. They had other reasons than their worldview for rejecting the Christian gospel. They were very much men of the world. Over recent centuries they had been deeply influenced by Hellenistic rationality and culture, and that, combined with the satisfaction of wielding religious and political power in the world as it was, induced in them worldly-mindedness and comparative laxity in matters of religion. They had wealth (they enjoyed massive revenues from the temple); they had power; they mixed in the highest circles (both Jewish and Gentile); they were educated and sophisticated. The world, as it was, was good enough for them. They could not see all that much wrong with it. As Paul would later say, they loved this present world. It was the only world they really believed in.

And here were these Christian apostles filling the heads of the masses with prophecy and the hope of a coming messianic kingdom, all based on their presupposition of the reality of resurrection. It offended their Hellenistic sense of rationality; it challenged their lifestyle, their worldview and their vested interests. And, above all, they were the men who as the ruling class were chiefly responsible for the judicial murder of Jesus. They could not afford to allow the preaching of the resurrection of Jesus to become widespread, and so they tried to suppress it by force (5:40).

The historical sequel was that the Christians defied them and suffered for it. Then in AD 70, the pagan Romans came and destroyed the temple; and from that time onward the one-time persecuting Sadducean party gradually sank into oblivion. The lesson should not be lost on our generation.

CHAPTER 5

Martyrdom or Fanaticism?

Many, perhaps all, of the great movements in history have had their martyrs; and many of the freedoms enjoyed and taken for granted today were won by men and women who were prepared to give their lives for the principles on which those freedoms are based. Who does not revere the memory of Socrates who died at the hands of ignorant superstition and political vested interests rather than abandon his uncompromising search for truth and justice?

The Christian church, too, has had a long list of martyrs. Jesus Christ himself was persecuted to death by the civil and religious authorities, and he taught his followers that persecution for his sake was an extreme honour and joy. It is no wonder, then, that Luke has devoted a great deal of space in Acts to Stephen, the first, and perhaps the greatest of all Christian martyrs. Understandably, the Christian church has revered his memory ever since.

But there are two things we should bear in mind about martyrs. First, true martyrs are not fanatics. Fanatics are just as liable to hound other people to death (by the million, if necessary) for opposing their beliefs as they are to die for them themselves. True martyrs kill nobody. Secondly, the way to truly honour martyrs is not simply to erect statues to them, or paint pictures of them, but to find out what they stood for, and then to stand for it ourselves.

What, then, were the principles for which Stephen was prepared to die, and why did his executioners think them so subversive as to merit execution?

To put it briefly, Stephen died for proclaiming that through Christ every person has the right of immediate and direct access to God without the need of any intermediary except Christ, and the right of knowing that through Christ they can here and now enjoy complete acceptance with God.

Put this way, it is perhaps difficult for us to see why anyone could have objected to what Stephen preached, let alone persecute him for it. But we must try to understand the historical situation. His opponents were the leading members of the Jewish hierarchy of priests in the national temple at Jerusalem; and they saw immediately that Stephen's Christian ideas would eventually make their temple, priesthood, and sacrifices unnecessary, irrelevant and obsolete. Hence their opposition.

Now of course they had a vested interest: the dues from the sacrifices offered by the local people and the thousands of international pilgrims made the high priest and his colleagues very wealthy men. But they were not motivated simply by the fear of financial loss. They honestly believed—and in this the Christians would have agreed with them—that the temple in Jerusalem, its sacrifices and priesthood had been set up by God's authority through the law of Moses in the Old Testament. They, therefore, charged Stephen with propagating the idea that Jesus Christ was going to destroy the temple, priesthood, and sacrifices which God himself had instituted. If proved, the charge carried a mandatory sentence of death for blasphemy.

Now Luke makes it clear from the start that Stephen had never said that Jesus Christ would physically destroy the Jerusalem temple. That part of the charge was false (Acts 6:11, 13, 14). But in another sense, there was a great deal of truth in what they said.

Consider the temple sin offerings. By their means, the Old Testament had taught the Israelites that sin against God (and all sin is ultimately against God) forfeits the life of the sinner. Sin's penalty must be paid before the sinner can be honourably forgiven. To find forgiveness the sinner had to bring an animal to the temple, confess his sins over its head, and kill it. The animal died as his substitute; the penalty was paid and the sinner forgiven.

Now Stephen and the other Christians agreed with the priests that this system was set up by God. They maintained, however, that it was self-evidently only symbolic. The death of animals could not in actual fact pay the penalty for human sin, as the Old Testament itself pointed out (Ps 40:6-7). They argued, therefore, that the system was never intended to be more than a temporary means of preparing people's minds for the death and sacrifice of Christ, the Lamb of God who should take away the sin of the world. This, too, the Old Testament had stated (Isa 53:5-12). The old system, then, was like a toy shop with toy candies and toy money which parents sometimes give their children to play with, so that when they grow up they will be prepared to discover that real candies have a price, and must be paid for with real money. Of course, when they reach that stage, toy money will be discarded.

The implications of this for the Jerusalem temple were, as the Jewish hierarchy rightly perceived, far-reaching. Their ancient system of sacrifices had never been more than a series of promissory notes which acknowledged, but could not actually pay, an ever-increasing debt. Now the death of Christ had paid that accumulated debt, and the old system could be abolished.

But the implications were even wider. Since Christ's sacrifice had paid the full penalty of all the sins of all who would thereafter believe on him, no other kind of sin offering would ever be necessary again. Nor would there be any need for Christ continually to repeat his own sacrifice, as the Jewish priests had been obliged constantly to repeat theirs (Heb 10:11–18).

But Stephen and the other New Testament writers were more radical still. They said that it was not only the temple sacrifices that were now obsolete: the temple itself was fast becoming obsolete as well (Heb 8:1–13). Christ himself had said the same while he was still on earth (John 4:19–24). And when he offered himself on the cross as the perfect sacrifice for sin, the historians tell us that something of major significance happened to the temple itself.

Like the tabernacle of Moses before it, the temple in Jerusalem was divided by a wall and a veil into two compartments. The inner compartment was called the Most Holy Place, and was a symbolic representation of heaven and of the immediate presence of God. Ordinary people were never allowed into that Most Holy Place. Only the high priest could go in, and that only once a year on the Day of Atonement. The point of this visual, architectural arrangement was, so the Bible tells us, to impress on the minds of the people that, as long as they were dependent on the constant sacrifices of animals, and ablutions in holy water, the way into God's immediate presence was for them not open (Heb 9:8-10).

But when Christ died on the cross, God himself tore down the veil in the temple (see Matt 27:50-51). By this symbolic act he indicated that, for all who put their faith in Christ, there is already unrestricted spiritual access into the immediate presence of God; and, in addition, a vigorous assurance of bodily access into God's presence in heaven at the second coming of Christ (Heb 10:19-22; John 14:1-3). For Stephen, the symbolism of the veil in the Jewish temple, therefore, was now obsolete, and, if retained, would deny the freedom proclaimed by the gospel.

But to the Jewish hierarchy, grounded in centuries of tradition, Stephen's views must have sounded completely heretical. His first task, therefore, was to try to convince the council that his views were not blasphemy against God—according to whose directions the original tabernacle had been built.

To prove this, Stephen pointed to the clear lesson of Old Testament history (Acts 7:2-53). Although God's overall purpose had always remained the same, there had been several distinct phases in his education of Israel for the coming of Messiah. Naturally, each phase superseded and left behind what had gone before. The child that has learned to count by playing with bricks will never be asked to abandon the laws of arithmetic; but he may rightly be called upon to give up the bricks and move on to computers. To refuse to move on would be disastrous.

So God had called Abraham out of the Gentiles, and told him and his son, Isaac, to stay in the promised land of Canaan (Acts 7:2-5; Gen 26:3). But later on, Isaac's son, Jacob, was told to take the whole tribe back among the Gentiles to Egypt (Acts 7:11-12; Gen 46:1-4). Then, some centuries later, Moses was sent to bring them out of Egypt back to Canaan once more (Acts 7:7-36). Through Moses, God had commanded Israel to build him a tabernacle, and to offer animal sacrifices. But, again after some centuries, God had indicated in the Psalms and Prophets that the animal sacrifices, the temple and the Aaronic priesthood would one day be superseded by something better (Pss 40 and 110; Isa 66:1-2).

There was, therefore, nothing blasphemous in Stephen's claim that, now that Jesus the Messiah had come, these old things had in fact been superseded by the promised better things. The real danger was that, just as their fathers before them had rejected Moses, the council would reject the Messiah and all these better things.

But the Jewish chief priests, faced with the great spiritual realities of the gospel of Christ, refused to give up their mere—and now obsolete—symbols, and they murdered Stephen for saying they should. Like their ancestors before them, they refused to keep pace with the living God; and all they were left with was a temple, full of symbols still, but deserted by the incarnate Son of God (Matt 23:37-38). In AD 70, God allowed the pagan Romans to come and raze it to the ground (Matt 24:2).

CHAPTER 6

Magic and the Gospel

In recent years we have witnessed an explosion of interest in religion, magic, the occult, astrology, and the paranormal. Men and women, finding themselves in a spiritual vacuum, are searching, sometimes in desperation, for some kind of spiritual experience which has been denied them by discredited materialistic philosophies. And yet, precisely because the search is sometimes so desperate, there is real danger of exploitation and fraud. For this reason Luke's next story is of great interest, for it shows us how to distinguish the false from the true.

Luke relates an encounter in Samaria between the Christian evangelist, Philip, and a certain man, Simon, whom Luke describes as practising a form of magic. Exactly what form of magic he practised, Luke does not tell us, but it was obviously very impressive, for the Samaritans were amazed by Simon's feats and, simply on that ground, felt convinced that his claims were true, and hailed him as 'the power of God that is called Great' (Acts 8:10).

And many people make a similar mistake nowadays. Because psychic and demonic powers are real (though often accompanied by a lot of superstition and gibberish), they unthinkingly suppose that they are spiritually healthy, and can be relied on to point us to the ultimate truth about God and the universe.

To complicate matters further, Luke tells us that, when Simon heard Philip preach and saw him perform miracles, he professed to believe the gospel and got himself baptized (8:13). But the sequel showed that he had not repented of his old magic. In fact, he had not even understood the gospel. To him, Christianity was simply another, and more powerful, form of magic, which he was quite happy to add to his repertoire.

This also happens in the modern world. In Mexico, for example, it is well known that many who have had themselves baptized as Christians, unrepentantly continue their pagan and demonic rites. And, unfortunately, at various times in history, Christian missionaries have deliberately assimilated pagan festivals into Christendom's religious calendar, in order (they claim) to make it easier for pagans to convert to Christianity. That is why, for instance, the local customs which surround the Feast of All Souls in some countries, strikingly resemble the customs practised at the Feast of Hungry Ghosts in places like Malaysia, when people visit the cemeteries and honour the spirits of their departed relatives.

This all raises the question: what, then, is the difference between true Christianity and magic? How can we distinguish the two? Some will say that there is no need to try. Jesus Christ and his apostles, they argue, did amazing miracles; so did Simon, and so do certain gurus nowadays. They are, therefore, all the same. Or they argue: Jesus claimed to be the Christ, the Son of God, and based his claim on his miracles; why shouldn't Simon or some modern guru equally claim to be the embodiment of some god, on the strength of their powers?

To argue like that is to make the mistake of confusing reality and truth. The fact that psychic powers are real, in the sense that they actually exist, does not necessarily mean that they are all healthy. All mushrooms are real; but some of them are deadly poison. Furthermore, the fact that spirits are real and can be contacted, does not mean that they necessarily tell the truth about God and the universe. In the underworld of international intrigue, spies are very real; but they cannot be relied on to tell the truth, except insofar as it furthers their deceit. Similarly, the Bible tells us, not all spirits are loyal to God. Indeed, it warns us not to believe every spirit, but to test the spirits whether they are of God: because many false prophets have gone out into the world (1 John 4:1).

It is in this connection that Luke describes for us the tell-tale signs which eventually exposed the fact that Simon was not a true believer in Christ, and that the kind of religion he represented was false and demonic.

First, there was his fundamentally false concept of the Holy Spirit. Observing that the Holy Spirit was given at[1] the laying on of the apostles' hands, he jumped to the conclusion that the apostles had discovered how to control the Holy Spirit, and could impart the Holy Spirit to

1. The Greek preposition which Luke uses means not 'through' but 'to the accompaniment of'.

whomever they wished. His conclusion was false. No man, not even an apostle, could control or impart the Holy Spirit. Only God can do that.

It was natural for Simon to think this way, for this is how all practitioners of magic and spiritism think. They profess to be able to control certain spirits. That is how they acquire their fame and status, for anyone who wishes to benefit from these powers must apply to them and depend on their techniques. So Simon, who doubtless had made a lot of money by his psychic performances, saw the opportunity of making a lot more, and so offered the apostles money to teach him this new technique of controlling and imparting the Holy Spirit.

In offering money to buy power, Simon made his second fundamental error. Luke explains: he thought he could 'obtain the gift of God with money'. This showed that he had not even begun to understand, let alone accept, the Christian gospel. The gift of the Holy Spirit is an integral part of salvation, and like salvation itself, is an utterly free gift that cannot be bought with money, or earned or merited in any way.[2] Simon's whole concept of God and of salvation was wrong. A spirit, the control of which can be bought for money, is self-evidently not the Holy Spirit of the almighty Creator. And a god who was prepared to give his Holy Spirit only to those who could afford to buy his salvation would obviously not be the God of infinite love, whose Spirit is, in fact, given freely and directly to all who will repent and believe.

2. See John 4:10; Acts 2:38; Eph 1:13–14; 2:8–9.

The third thing that showed Simon to be a fraud was his extravagant claim to be that power of God which is called The Great Power. In the same way, a modern New Age pantheist like Shirley MacLaine not only claims to be in tune with the basic powers of the universe, but asserts 'I AM THAT I AM' (which is one way in which the Bible speaks of almighty God himself), and encourages others to follow her techniques, with the hope that they too one day will be able to claim the same thing. This is none other than the Satanic lie whispered into mankind's ear in the garden of Eden: 'You will be like God'; but it holds its fatal fascination still.

How different all of this is from Jesus Christ. True, he claimed to be the Son of God, and supported his claim by doing miracles. But of him it is said that

> Though he was in the form of God, did not consider equality with God a thing to be grasped, but emptied himself, by taking the form of a servant, being born in the likeness of men. And being found in human form, he humbled himself by becoming obedient to the point of death, even death on a cross. (Phil 2:6-8)

In fact, Jesus is the one who, as Luke is about to remind us in his very next story, fulfilled the Old Testament prophecy of Isaiah by becoming God's Suffering Servant: the lamb led to the slaughter, and silent before the shearers—the crucified Christ who was wounded for our transgressions, who was bruised for our iniquities, and by whose stripes we are healed (see Isa 53). It is by first becoming God's humble, suffering and redeeming Servant, and then by being raised from the dead—and not simply by doing a few miracles—that Jesus Christ has been demonstrated to be God's unique Son. Between him and the boasting Simons of this world, there is no comparison.

How, then, did the Samaritans come to be deceived by a man like Simon? The answer is: as a result of their neglect—indeed, their positive rejection—of large parts of the Old Testament. Before Israel entered Canaan, God had warned them that they were not to erect temples all over the land, but only one; and that one, as he subsequently indicated, was to be in Jerusalem. The reason given was that if they offered their sacrifices just anywhere, they would fall victims to the polytheistic superstitions of their Canaanite neighbours.

Now the Samaritans of the first century AD accepted the first five books of the Bible. But, for all kinds of reasons too detailed and complicated to discuss here, they had rejected all the rest; and especially those parts which appointed Jerusalem as the place where God's temple should be situated, and as the city to which the Messiah would eventually come as king. Instead, they made Samaria the centre of their worship and, in doing so, fell into the snare of polytheistic superstition, as God's Word had warned them they would.

Now when they heard Philip preach the gospel and they believed it, they were, Luke tells us, filled with joy. But how could they now be sure that Philip was a genuine messenger of God, and not some religious charlatan or emissary of Satan? And how could they be sure that their spiritual experience was genuine, and not just another deception propagated by some spurious cult or sect? The answer is simple: to stop people from being deceived, God himself had prepared for the coming of the Christ by predicting in the Old Testament that he would come of the Jewish nation; that Jerusalem would be his capital city; that he would be rejected by his nation and die for the sins of the world just outside Jerusalem; he then would be raised from the dead. And the Saviour whom Philip preached to the Samaritans was precisely this Christ, who fulfilled those Old Testament predictions.

This is why God made the Samaritans submit to the laying on of hands by the apostles from Jerusalem before he gave them his Holy Spirit. This procedure was quite abnormal: people normally received the Holy Spirit the moment they repented and believed, as we see from the famous example in Acts 10. But the Samaritans were a special case. For their own good and assurance, they had to be brought to realize and admit that the only genuine spiritual experience of salvation is that which comes through faith in the gospel that historically was first preached by the Christian apostles from Jerusalem; through faith, that is, in the Christ of God who died for our sins according to the Old Testament Scriptures, was buried, and rose again the third day according to the Scriptures, just outside the city of Jerusalem.

Still today that remains the indispensable mark of the true gospel, and the only basis of true spiritual experience.

CHAPTER 7

The True Meaning of Conversion

It is evident on every page of Luke's history that early Christianity spread by making converts. Not so obvious, perhaps, today, is what the term conversion really means; for in the intervening centuries the matter has become confused.

In the Dark Ages, for instance, pagan kings, professing conversion to Christianity, sometimes compelled their subjects to submit to baptism, since they thought that simply performing this rite on people immediately turned them all, willing or unwilling, into Christians. More extreme methods were used at a later date. Jews in Spain, for example, were given the choice of converting to Christianity or being burned at the stake. But this kind of thing is not what early Christianity understood by conversion. All forced conversion, whether to a religion or to a political ideology, is, of course, tyrannously evil. Forced conversion to Christianity is, in addition, a contradiction in terms. For Christianity insists on the integrity of the individual's moral judgment and freedom of choice.

A second confusion that arose in post-apostolic times was that if a nation or a family converted to Christianity, its descendants did not themselves need to be converted: they were automatically Christians, and remained so, unless they personally opted out.

A third, much more general confusion nowadays, is that all people everywhere, being creatures of God, are also children of God and need no conversion. But Christ himself drew a sharp distinction between physical birth—by which we become creatures of God, and spiritual re-birth—by which we become children of God. We have no choice in our physical birth; but, according to Christ, our spiritual re-birth is only possible by conscious, personal repentance and acceptance of him as Saviour and Lord (see 1 John 1:8–9; 3:1–16).

In this connection, Luke's narrative is particularly instructive. He not only tells us that, from time to time, crowds of people got converted; but at Acts 8:4–9:30 he relates the conversions of two very different individuals, one a pagan polytheist from Ethiopia, and the other a deeply religious Jewish monotheist. Both needed, and both experienced, conversion. Luke's detailed, slow-motion picture allows us to see the crucial stages in their spiritual re-births.

The first element in the polytheist's conversion was the sheer attractiveness of Israel's monotheistic faith. Israel's God was the creator and upholder of the universe; paganism's many gods were little more than personifications and deifications of the blind forces and processes of nature. Israel's God was transcendent above all the matter and forces of the universe; and man, being made in his image, was likewise superior to them in significance. In paganism, mortal men were little more than the slaves, or else the toys, of the gods—doomed to be discarded when the gods lost interest in them, or abandoned to their fate which even the gods could not resist. The Ethiopian had understandably tired of these absurdities; and just before the Christian evangelist Philip met him, he had been up to Jerusalem to seek and to worship God in the Jewish temple.

Now, turning from polytheism—or, for that matter, from atheism—to believe in the existence of the one true God, is obviously a necessary first step in conversion. But it is not the whole story; for by itself it leaves unanswered the all-important question: how can man approach God, and find a right and satisfactory personal relationship with him?

The next element, then, in the Ethiopian's conversion was his personal search for God by reading the Bible. In Jerusalem, apparently, he had obtained a copy of the Old Testament prophecy of Isaiah, which eloquently spoke of God's plan for the redemption, not only of Israel, but of all mankind. That redemption, so Isaiah predicted, would be achieved by a great messianic figure called the Servant of the Lord, whom God would send into the world. He would reign as universal king, put down evil, banish war, establish worldwide justice and peace, bring salvation to Israel and to the nations, and eventually restore the whole creation.

This hope, guaranteed as it was by the love, rationality, and power of the Creator, had nothing to match it in paganism. But, even more striking was the prediction that this messianic figure would himself suffer rejection, torture, and death as the means of achieving the promised redemption! What could it mean?

When Philip met him, the Ethiopian had reached the very passage in Isaiah that predicted Messiah's innocent, non-retaliatory sufferings: 'Like a sheep he was led to the slaughter and like a lamb before its shearers is silent, so he opens not his mouth. In his humiliation justice was denied him . . . his life is taken away from the earth' (Acts 8:32-33, citing Isa 53:7-8). Philip was able to tell the Ethiopian not only that these prophecies referred to Jesus, but that they had been fulfilled by him, and that his resurrection from the dead had shown that Jesus, the innocent sufferer, was in fact the promised Messiah-King, Son of God, and Redeemer.

Millions have felt the power of this story of Jesus, the divine King who suffered innocently and without retaliation; who even prayed for those who crucified him. But what exactly does this mean for us, and for the world at large? Is its implication that, if only everyone in the world were to follow the example of Christ and accept without retaliation the suffering that comes upon them through their own sins and those of other people, then, by accepting this suffering, the whole world would be redeemed?

It is certainly true that once people become disciples of Christ, they are called on to follow Christ's example and, in life's various situations, to suffer without retaliation (1 Pet 2:21-24). But we must face the realities of this fallen world.

The two thousand years since the death and resurrection of Christ have shown unfortunately that it is an altogether unrealistic hope that evil, if not retaliated against, will, like a hurricane, blow itself out and become a spent force. Nor, of course, can the mere non-retaliatory sufferings of the innocent in the present or the future redress the injustices of the past. Indeed, the Bible plainly says that only the second coming of Christ in power, to execute the judgments of God on this evil world and to establish his own universal kingdom, can do that. The reality of the situation is that, until men and women are converted, they will have neither the power nor the willingness to follow Christ's example of suffering.

What, then, is the relation of his suffering to conversion? To find out, we must follow Philip's exposition of the gospel all the way. Beginning with the verses that spoke of the non-retaliatory sufferings of Christ (because that is the place that the Ethiopian had reached in his reading), Philip would certainly have gone on to expound the remaining verses of that prophecy. They spoke of those deeper substitutionary sufferings of Christ, by which individual men and women can be reconciled to their Creator. According to Isaiah, it was not to be by following Christ's example and by suffering ourselves, that we were to obtain forgiveness, peace with God, and eternal life. 'The punishment that brought us peace was upon him', says the prophet—not upon us. It is by his wounds, not by our own, that we are healed.

We all like sheep have gone astray, and the Lord has laid the iniquity of us all on him, not on us. God will make his soul a sacrifice for sin, said the prophet; and the metaphor he used, drawn as it was from ancient Israel's symbolic sacrificial system, put the matter beyond doubt. When an ancient Israelite brought an innocent animal as his sin offering, the animal died, not as an example of how the sinner might in turn suffer for his own sins and thus find forgiveness; it died as a substitute in the place of the sinner, so that the sinner should not himself have to suffer the penalty of sin and die.

The doctrine of reconciliation with God through the substitutionary sufferings of Christ has not always appealed to everyone as good news. It is difficult for our pride to accept that we are sinners in need of salvation. But if we can gain, or contribute to, our salvation by suffering for our own sins, and for the sins of others, it salvages at least some of our pride.

Yet human pride and independence of God are the root of our trouble; no paradise can be achieved until they are eradicated. It is when we come to see and to accept that we are nothing but spiritual bankrupts, who can only be forgiven solely by God's grace through the substitutionary sufferings of His Son, that the root of our pride is cut, and our relationship with God is transformed. So it was with the Ethiopian who on these terms was converted, had himself baptized, and went on his way rejoicing.

In that very same chapter of Isaiah that led to the Ethiopian's conversion, the prophet had predicted that by his knowledge God's righteous Servant the Messiah would justify many (Isa 53:11); and the second case of individual conversion which Luke here records is that of Saul of Tarsus, the man who later, as the Apostle Paul, wrote so extensively on the fundamental Christian doctrine of justification by faith. He learned the meaning of justification and its necessity, not only from the Bible but from his own personal experience.

All his life he had been a strict monotheist and a deeply religious man, who had made an honest (and, as he felt, successful) attempt to keep God's moral and religious law. Indeed, it was his zeal for God that made him persecute the Christians for what he considered their blasphemous claim that Jesus was equal with God! But when the risen Lord appeared to him on the road from Jerusalem to Damascus, it produced three radical revolutions in his thought and behaviour.

First, it exposed the fact that in spite of his strict monotheism—he had always believed in the existence of one true God—in the only sense that really mattered, he was not a believer in God at all, and never had been! The Jesus whom he had been persecuting, he now knew to be God Incarnate; thus his own actions had demonstrated him to be not only an unbeliever, but an enemy of God.

Secondly, it exposed the fact that all his effort to keep God's law was worthless. It had ended in his murder of God's Son! He was as lost as any pagan polytheist. He now saw with blinding clarity that if ever he was going to be justified and accepted by God, it would have to be solely on the grounds of faith; where faith meant, as he later expressed it, 'being justified freely by God's grace, man is justified by faith apart from observing the law. To the man who does not work but trusts God who justifies the wicked, his faith is credited as righteousness' (see Rom 3:24–4:5).

Thirdly, his conversion had a momentous outcome. Before his conversion, when he believed that salvation depended on his merit, he was a self-centred, persecuting bigot, who cared nothing for the salvation of the world outside Judaism. But when he discovered that salvation is not by merit but by faith, he never persecuted anyone again. On the contrary, he became the greatest of all the early Christian missionaries. It is no exaggeration to say that through his oral and written exposition of the doctrine of justification by faith multi-millions throughout the whole world, up to the present day, have found spiritual freedom and peace with God.

CHAPTER 8

The True Internationalism

Racism is surely one of the worst evils that has ever afflicted mankind. There is perhaps a spark of instinctive racial pride in every one of us, even if it never breaks out into discrimination against minorities, positive persecution or so-called ethnic cleansing. But not so long ago racism, deliberately formalized into a rigorous system of political thought, engulfed Europe and Asia in a hideous conflagration.

The first stage came in the nineteenth century with thinkers like de Gobineau of France who held that of the three principal races in the world, only the white was truly noble; and that among the whites the Aryan race was supreme.

Then came James Hunt, founder of the London Anthropological Society. He taught that the moral and intellectual aspects of a person were as much racial qualities as were the size and shape of the cranium; that all racial qualities were innate and unchangeable; and that therefore belief in the 'equality of all mankind' was an unscientific prejudice which should be abandoned.

To this already dangerous brew, thinkers like Vacher de Lapouge of France and Otto Ammon of Germany added the deadly poison of social Darwinism. They proclaimed it to be a law of nature that, in the struggle of life, races with the fittest qualities survived and become dominant, while other weaker races were subdued or eliminated. To them it was self-evident that the Aryan race was the fittest in every way and so had been predestined by the irresistible deterministic laws of the universe to be supreme over all others.

The result of such theories was an immediate, catastrophic devaluation of human beings generally. Since human life was no longer believed to have been created in the image of God, it was not regarded as sacred. Millions could rightly be eliminated, without ground for complaint. It was nature's law that only the fittest should survive.

Finally came theoreticians like the notorious Germanized Englishman, H. S. Chamberlain. He it was who preached that the Jewish race was evil and a threat to world society; and that the Germans were the chosen people destined by nature to eliminate that threat. Such ideas intoxicated and deranged Hitler, with results which we know only too well.

Now anti-Semitism is not the only evil to which racism has given rise; but it has been, unfortunately, an all too frequent blot on the history of Christendom. It is true that from its inception, as Luke's history shows, Christianity was obliged to diverge from Judaism over a number of fundamental issues, and in particular over the matter of race. In Judaism, race was vitally important; in Christianity, irrelevant. In order to understand this difference, however, we must first try to see why the question of race was (and is) so significant for the Jews; and then we must allow Luke to show us why, and in what sense, the Christian gospel proclaims that in Christ 'there is neither Jew nor Greek, . . . for you are all one in Christ Jesus' (Gal 3:28).

The nation of Israel (they were only called Jews later in history) was a comparative late-comer among the nations of the ancient world. But from the start, the nation claimed—according to the Old Testament—to be a special race, destined not by the automatic, deterministic forces of social Darwinism, but by the Creator himself to play a unique role in history. The claim is credible; for throughout many centuries Israel was, in one particular, literally unique. All the other nations, however brilliant in civilized arts, administration and engineering, were sunk in the demeaning absurdities of polytheism, worshipping the deified forces of nature, the sun god, the moon god, the god of fertility and such like.

By vivid contrast, Israel—and not just a few advanced thinkers among them but the nation as a whole—stood out solitary and distinct in its witness to the one true God, transcendent above the universe and all its forces, the Creator and sustainer of all. It is understandable, then, that Israel should have considered their monotheism superior to the other nations' animism and polytheism; but their monotheistic doctrine, unlike the theory of Aryan superiority, did not imply that the Israelites were a super-race. Quite the opposite. Israel's Old Testament doctrine of creation taught that all men everywhere, of whatever race, are creatures of God, made in his image. In that respect all are equal; every individual and every race, even the weakest and not just the fittest, is equally valuable and significant. All human life is sacred.

Moreover the Old Testament repeatedly asserts that God's call to Israel to fill their unique role in history was not given to Israel primarily for Israel's own sake, but so that through Israel all the other nations of the earth should eventually be blessed. One day through Israel God would send the Jewish Messiah to be the Saviour of the world, and when he came millions of Gentiles would find salvation through him.

Meanwhile, to the Jew, membership of this unique race with its unique role was all important. If Gentiles converted from paganism to faith in God, they could of course be adopted, so to speak, into the Jewish race. But for that to happen, males had to undergo the Jewish rite of circumcision, the badge of spiritual, if not physical, descent from Abraham, the ancestor of the Jewish race; and both men and women had to submit to the Jewish food laws and purity laws, which made unrestricted social contact with other Gentiles difficult if not impossible. Some submitted, like Helena, the Queen of Adiabane, and her son Izates. But many others deeply resented it, for it seemed a form of bigoted religious racism which held that Jews were inherently better than all other races.

It was not so, of course. Parents who forbid their teenage daughter to attend parties where some use drugs are not saying that their daughter is inherently better than other teenagers. They are admitting that she is inherently just as weak as the rest, and if not protected from mixing with drug addicts, might well succumb to peer pressure.

So it was with God and Israel. The Gentile world around them was rife with every kind of sexual perversion; with infanticide; with deceit; with commercial, social and political oppression; with cruelty and murder. God therefore set up the food and purity laws to act as perimeter defences around the Jews to protect the inner citadel of Judaism's social and religious values. The constant complaint of their own Old Testament prophets is that when Israel disregarded those laws, it led to compromise with decadent Gentile practices, and to moral and spiritual disaster.

It was, then, no insignificant matter when, as Luke tells us, the early Christians, themselves Jews, abandoned these defences, these rules and regulations. They did not, of course, abandon Israel's monotheism or the moral standards of Israel's law. But they did abandon Israel's preoccupation with the special privileges of their race. They tore down the barriers between Jew and Gentile, and declared that, through Christ, God was doing a new thing in the world. He was reconciling both Jew and Gentile, first to himself and then to one another through one and the selfsame Christ. He was creating a 'new man,' a worldwide fellowship in which race was irrelevant and mutual love reigned instead of hostility (see Eph 2).

The worldwide implications of this change were momentous; and Luke was not slow to recognize them. He has in fact devoted a whole section of his history to describing the incident that proved the catalyst in provoking the change (Acts 10:1–11:18).

The first things to go were the food laws and the ritual purity regulations which inhibited social fellowship between Jew and Gentile. Christ himself had pointed out that external ritual washings are, after all, only symbols. They cannot touch or cleanse the corruption of the human heart; but they can, and often do, become a substitute morally, and blind a person's eyes to his real moral and spiritual uncleanness. Christ therefore, with divine authority, abolished the food laws and the ritual purity regulations (Mark 7:1-23). And when the apostle Peter was invited by a devout Roman centurion to visit him in his home to explain the Christian gospel, God intervened with a vivid object lesson to confirm to Peter directly that he was now free to go and eat with Gentiles.

Then God taught Peter another, more fundamental, lesson. Many Jews had fallen into the trap of thinking that, in spite of their personal and national sins, their privileged role meant that they were by definition better than Gentiles; and that, however noble and morally upright individual Gentiles were, nevertheless, being Gentiles, they were by definition unclean and unholy. Peter had to be taught that there are no such first class and second class human beings: no one, whatever his race, is to be regarded by definition as common or unclean (Acts 10:28).

Already, then, these two lessons had prepared Peter the Jew and his Jewish friends to come and stand side by side with Gentiles on the platform of their common humanity. But it was the gospel of Jesus—the crucified and risen Son of God—that welded their Jewish and Gentile hearts together. It is at the foot of the cross of Christ that Jews and Gentiles discover their common guilt. That cross declares that, whether we have sinned much or little, there is no difference between any of us in this respect, that all have sinned and do come short of the glory of God. We can be justified, but only through God's unmerited grace made available to us through Christ and the redemption achieved by his sacrifice for sin. The cross of Christ, by the very salvation it offers us, proclaims all of us morally bankrupt, with no grounds for boasting one over the other (Rom 3:21-31).

It is through the resurrection of Christ that Jew and Gentile also discover who their common judge will be (Acts 10:42) and their common need of salvation. And it is through the resurrection of Christ that Jews and Gentiles can receive forgiveness of sins on exactly the same terms, namely, by simple, direct, personal faith in the living Lord Jesus (10:43).

There was more. When Cornelius and his Gentile friends put their faith in Jesus, God gave them his Holy Spirit in the same way as he had earlier done to Peter and his fellow Jewish believers (11:15-18). To their surprise and then to their exuberant joy, these Jews and Gentiles found that they were now sharing a common life, nothing less than the life of the Holy Spirit dwelling within them which automatically formed them into a spiritual unity, one body in the Lord. This was for them an immediate end of racism, the dawn of true internationalism.

Still today this is the basis and this the power of that worldwide unity that binds together all true believers in Christ, regardless of race. And it is this same power of the indwelling Holy Spirit, rather than a system of food laws, rituals, rites, and social segregation, that enables true believers to resist the pressures of a sinful world and to live a life of genuine and increasing holiness.

All too realistically, however, this glorious slice of history from Luke's Acts ends on a sombre note. Judaism's orthodox establishment at Jerusalem was dismayed at the way the Christians were seemingly throwing away Jewish privileges and uniting with Gentiles without requiring Gentiles to become Jews. The establishment therefore connived with Herod when he used his political power to ban and persecute the Christian leaders and preachers (12:23). This, however, is no ground for Christians to feel superior to those ancient Jews. From time to time in the course of the centuries, decadent Christianity has itself used the same tactics against those whom it has considered to be its enemies. The better reaction would be first to learn from Luke what true Christianity is, and then, embracing it, to renounce all racism of every kind and all attempts at political discrimination on the ground of religion.

CHAPTER 9

The Fight against
Religious Oppression

One of the ugliest features in the history of our sorry world has surely been misery and oppression caused by religion. Atheists have often and rightly pointed out that, as the ancient Roman poet Lucretius put it, 'again and again religion has given birth to sinful and unholy deeds'.[1] The particular barbarity cited by Lucretius was Agamemnon's sacrifice of his virgin daughter Iphigenia on the altar of the pagan goddess Artemis, in order to gain that goddess's favour. But pagan superstitions have not been the only, or the worst, culprits. Christendom has its shameful record too: crusades by so-called Christian nations against infidels, and myriad burnings and torturings of supposed heretics, all of it in plain defiance of Christ's own prohibition on the use of violence to further or protect his kingdom (see John 18:36-37). In England, at various times professing Christian

---

1. *De Rerum Natura*, Book 1, ll. 82–83.

monarchs even had people burned at the stake for possessing and reading the words of Christ in the Bible!

The Bible itself, of course, protests against this kind of thing as loudly as any atheist. Christ himself lamented his own Jewish nation's long history of persecuting the prophets; he drove out of the temple those who were exploiting religion for the purpose of making money and thereby oppressing the poor; he denounced certain religious professionals (Pharisees) who seemed outwardly to be holy men but inwardly were morally corrupt; and then with utter impartiality he warned his disciples that from time to time there would arise in his own kingdom and church, men in high office who would beat their fellow servants and live immoral and self-indulgent lives (Luke 12:45–46). The fact is that religion in the hands of men who have never experienced personal regeneration can often foment the worst features of fallen human nature; though, to be fair, political ideology, when adopted as a quasi-religious faith, has often provided hideous examples of the same kind of thing.

Serious as all these scandals are, however, they are self-evidently corruptions of true religion. More dangerous, because not so self-evidently wrong, are doctrines and practices which appear to be religiously respectable, but which, if adopted, would turn the very gospel of Christ into a form of spiritual slavery, less lurid than other perversions such as we have just considered, but fundamentally more serious. Indeed, in the next section of Acts (12:25–16:5) it is one of Luke's major concerns to record the reaction of the apostles to early attempts to incorporate such doctrines and practices into Christianity.

Luke tells us (15:5) that certain 'believers' (though in what sense they were believers he does not say—presumably they believed that Jesus was the Christ, the Son of God; and that, of course, was good!) began so to misconstrue the terms and conditions of salvation, that Peter declared that their teaching would put 'a yoke on the neck of the disciples which neither our fathers nor we have been able to bear'. Peter regarded the imposition of such spiritual slavery on people, when the whole purpose of the gospel is to set people free, to be tantamount to 'putting God to the test' (15:10). Strong words! But they are matched by the fervour of Paul's appeal to the Christians in Galatia when they were subsequently troubled by similar misrepresentations of the gospel: 'For freedom Christ has set us free; stand firm therefore, and do not submit again to a yoke of slavery' (Gal 5:1).

In this connection Luke first gives us a summary of what Paul preached in the Jewish synagogue at Pisidian Antioch on the topic of salvation (Acts 13:14-41). Paul makes it clear that what God is offering mankind through Jesus Christ is primarily a salvation that sets people free: 'God has brought to Israel a Saviour, Jesus . . . to us has been sent the message of this salvation. . . . "that you may bring salvation to the ends of the earth"' (13:23, 26, 47).

But salvation in what sense? To illustrate his point, Paul reminds them that their nation had already experienced God's salvation at various levels. When they had been forced to work as aliens without civil rights in the slave labour camps of ancient Egypt, salvation had meant being set free from tyrannous economic, social, and political oppression. It also meant freedom for self-determination as a nation, and freedom to worship and serve God according to their conscience. Later, when compromise with the idolatry, immorality, and vice of the surrounding nations eventually brought them under their domination, salvation had meant liberation from the enslaving consequences of their own sinful practices and disobediences against God.

So now with Jesus Christ, the descendant of Israel's prototypical deliverer, King David: salvation meant liberation and freedom. But from what?

First of all from mankind's universal enemy, death (13:32–37). For what is the ultimate sense of existence, if all our social and political freedoms, all our progress to a new world order, only advance each individual, each nation, each civilization, and the whole universe to the emotional and intellectual frustration of universal, meaningless death? By the resurrection of Jesus Christ, God has demonstrated that the universe is not a closed system of internal cause and effect. One day it will be restored and set free from its bondage to decay and corruption.

Marvellously good news, then—but many people do not feel it so. Instinct tells them (and the Bible confirms) that if there is going to be a resurrection of all mankind, there will also be a final judgment. There must be. The idea that God would raise all mankind to a glorious eternal life and simply ignore the sins and injustices committed in this life is self-evidently a fairy tale, devoid of moral sense. But it is this fear of having to stand one day before God as judge that makes religion seem to many people oppressive, so that they prefer to think that there will be no resurrection. Paul knew it well; the congregation in the synagogue at Antioch had their own personal reasons, as we all have, for fearing a judgment after death; but in addition, their fellow-countrymen in Jerusalem and their religious leaders had crucified Jesus out of religious animosity. His resurrection, they must have felt, would carry implications too awful to contemplate.

It is in this historical context, then, that the relevance of the second element in salvation is most clearly seen. No reiteration of the demands of the law on God's part could have changed the hostility in hearts that had crucified his Son. No promise on the people's part to try to keep God's law in future could have wiped out the guilt of their sin and made it possible for God justly to forgive them. The gospel is this: that God himself undertook the task of removing this spiritual impasse.

At this pivotal point in world history God used the occasion of man's hostility against his Son to do what the Old Testament prophets had foretold he would do (13:27-35). In his love, God, in the person of his Son, took upon himself the penalty of human sin which his holiness demanded, paid it by his own suffering, thus making forgiveness possible for all who would repent and believe. And not only forgiveness—for that could be construed as simply forgiveness for this or that particular sin or even the single sin of crucifying Christ—but 'justification from all things'; which, whatever it means, is said to be something that no one could attain to, not even by the most sincere efforts to keep God's law given through Moses (13:39).

When we say that someone's action was justified, we are declaring that he was right to do what he did, and that we approve of his action. Again, if someone is accused of a crime and at the trial the court justifies him, it means that the court declares him to be innocent of the charge brought against him. But when the Bible says that God justifies those who believe, it clearly does not mean that God approves of everything they have done or even that God regards most of their life as having been on the whole acceptable. And it certainly does not mean that God regards them as innocent; for God declares all to be guilty sinners.

What does the word 'justify' mean, then, in the Bible? The famous statement in the New Testament that God 'justifies the ungodly' (Rom 4:5) quite obviously does not mean that God regards ungodliness as innocent, or even as generally acceptable, behaviour. Does it then mean, perhaps, that God makes the ungodly man just, by changing him and gradually turning him from a sinner into 'a good-living person'? No! God certainly does that for everyone who truly believes; but in the Bible the process by which he does it is called, not justification, but sanctification. And the difference in meaning is not a matter of splitting hairs. Sanctification is necessarily a long drawn-out process, involving much effort on man's part and often considerable suffering. And such are God's standards of holiness that in all realism he reminds us that we shall never be perfect in this life. At life's end, we shall still merit his verdict: 'all have sinned [in the past] and [still do] fall short of the glory of God [in the present]' (Rom 3:23).

If then our acceptance with God depended on our progress in holiness, no one could be sure in this life of final acceptance with God; and no one with any concept of God's standards would dare to presume it. And since for a person not to enjoy acceptance with God is the ultimate disaster, the attempt to gain that acceptance by progress in holiness, dogged by constant and inevitable awareness of having come short, would turn the whole procedure into an oppressively impossible task, into a kind of slavery. It would be like telling a teenager who had taken his father's brand new car without permission and wrecked it in an accident, that he must restore it to its original perfection, and that, not until the restoration was complete, could he be sure of his father's unrestrained love, forgiveness, and acceptance. A conscientious boy would be oppressively burdened by what would be, for him, such an impossible task. A less conscientious boy would turn into a rebel. These are precisely the positions that many people find themselves in with God!

How different it would be if the father first assured the boy that he was already completely forgiven and that his acceptance did not depend on his success in repairing the car; but that, in the confidence of being already accepted, he was expected to co-operate with his father in repairing the car, and to do so more and more as he grew older. That is exactly what God does for people when in the biblical sense of the word he justifies them. Justification is not the long, drawn-out process of putting the wreckage of our lives right. It is the instantaneous declaration made by God the moment a person repents and believes, that God forgives him and accepts him now and for ever; that God's acceptance does not depend on that person's success in putting the wreckage right; he is already clear, now and for ever, of any charge that God's holy law could bring against him; but in that confidence he is expected in fellowship with God to begin the long process of developing a holy life.

But, says someone, How can that be? How can God declare a man to be quit of any charge that God's law could bring against him while the man himself, however sincere, is still a sinner and far from perfect? The principle according to which God can do this is enunciated by Paul in his Letter to the Romans (6:7); only we must once more be careful to translate Paul's Greek exactly. What he says is (literally translated): 'The man who has died has been justified from sin.'

Suppose a country in which murder is a capital offence. As long as a murderer lived, he would stand under the law's condemnation and be liable to its penalty. But once he is executed and has paid the law's penalty, he is justified, and he passes out of the law's jurisdiction for ever. Now the penalty of our sin against God was eternal separation from God, that is, eternal death. We could never come to the end of paying that penalty if we had to pay it ourselves. But what we could never do, God has done for us in Christ. For all who put their faith in Christ, God is graciously prepared to count Christ's death as their death; and so for them the law's penalty is paid and they can be declared justified.

But how is it just that an innocent party—Christ—should suffer the law's penalty for other people's sins? The answer is that, in that sense, it is not a question of Christ dying for other people's sins. For now, consider what believing in Christ involves. It does not mean simply believing that Jesus is the Son of God. It means becoming one with him. Just as marriage makes a man and woman physically one, so, the Bible explains, whoever puts faith in Christ and receives him becomes spiritually one with him (1 Cor 6:17). For Christ is not just one more human being. He is the God–Man, the great representative man, who incorporates into himself all who trust him. In death he bore their sins and paid their penalty; risen from the dead, he shares with them his resurrection life. Joined to him, they are accepted by God as fully as he is, and given the permanent status of children of God. And here lies the secret of how it is that justification by faith does not lead thereafter to irresponsible and lax living. The believer finds himself joined in a practical, living partnership with Christ, with new motives and new power to pursue progressive holiness.

But it has proved notoriously difficult for some people, when the gospel speaks of justification by faith, to grasp what 'faith' means in this context. This was, for instance, the difficulty that according to Luke lay behind the dispute in the early churches, to which we earlier referred. Some Jews who had come to believe that Jesus was the Christ, the Son of God, still felt that the initiatory rite of circumcision followed by the keeping of the law of Moses was absolutely necessary for salvation (Acts 15:1, 5). And since then many people, thinking that baptism is the Christian equivalent of Jewish circumcision, have maintained that baptism and the keeping of God's law are necessary and indispensable conditions for being saved. The inevitable result of believing this: no one can know in this life that they are accepted with God, since no one can know that they have kept God's law well enough to do what is in fact impossible anyway, namely to qualify for salvation. And so, as Peter declared, they turn the very gospel of freedom into a yoke of bondage. Luke, being the perceptive historian he was, saw how crucial this debate was for the very survival of the Christian gospel, and carefully recorded, for all time, the unanimous freedom-giving verdict of all the apostles: 'We believe that we will be saved [not by circumcision and the keeping of the law but] through the grace of the Lord Jesus' (15:11).

CHAPTER 10

The Inviolability of the Human Personality

Somewhere around the year AD 49, Paul, the Christian apostle, took a momentous step fraught with immeasurable consequences for the whole Western world. He crossed over from Asia and, for the first time, preached the gospel in a European city. Almost at once he ran into trouble. There was in the city a group of businessmen who owned, or at least managed, a female spirit-medium. Paul exorcised the spirit, which put an end to the fees which the businessmen received from the public for consultations with the medium. Whereupon, with the support of the infuriated crowd, they hauled Paul and his colleague, Silas, before the magistrates. 'These men', they alleged, 'are Jews and are throwing our city into an uproar by advocating customs unlawful for us as Romans to accept or practice.'

Faced with civil commotion, the magistrates did not wait to conduct a proper investigation: they had the Christian missionaries publicly stripped, severely flogged, and then thrown into a high-security cell in the local prison (Acts 16:11–40).

Now obviously loss of income is enough to account for the opposition of the businessmen; but it will hardly explain the fury of the crowd, who in other circumstances might not necessarily have been all that upset by the sight of wealthy businessmen suffering a reduction in their income. The fact is that the arrival of the Christian missionaries touched three areas of their lives in a way which, they instinctively felt, threatened their personal identity and security. And since the gospel can still affect people in this way, it will be worthwhile analysing these causes in detail.

First, there was national culture. The city of Philippi, though situated in Macedonia, was a Roman colony, independent of the surrounding provincial administration, with a government organization modelled on Rome itself. Its citizens were not only Europeans; they were also citizens of Rome, and very proud of it. They dressed like Romans and often spoke Latin rather than Greek.

And the missionaries were not only Asiatics; they were Jews! The very idea that Asiatic Jews should imagine that they could teach the European Roman citizens of Philippi anything was felt as an insult to their superior Western culture (which, incidentally, is ironic; for nowadays in many Asiatic countries Asian people regard the gospel as a Western religion and an insult to their superior Asiatic culture!).

But more than that: in a vast international cosmopolitan society such as the Roman empire had become, people would have clung to their own national culture as a means of asserting their individual personal identity, and of not being lost in a meaningless, uniform sea of humanity. People still feel the same way today. And where a totalitarian government has suppressed local culture, as Franco for many years suppressed Catalan language and literature in Spain, it is understandable that, when the suppression is removed, local national culture should re-assert itself and resent the intrusion of alien culture.

Moreover, one has to admit that, in many parts of the world, visiting Christian preachers have often failed to distinguish between the fundamental truths of the gospel and the cultural trappings, music, architecture, style of presentation and so forth that have collected around it in their home countries. In so doing, they have confused the gospel itself in the minds of their foreign audience and unnecessarily provoked resentment.

But Paul was keenly aware of this danger. His own sensitive respect for other people's culture is shown in a letter which he subsequently wrote to another Greek city:

> Though I am free from all, I have made myself a servant to all, that I might win more of them. To the Jews I became as a Jew . . . To those under the [Mosaic] law I became as one under the law . . . To those outside the [Mosaic] law I became as one outside the law (not being outside the law of God but under the law of Christ) . . . I have become all things to all people, that by all means I might save some. (1 Cor 9:19–22)

We may be sure, then, that Paul would not have attacked or tried to suppress anything that was good and wholesome in the Philippians' culture, nor have tried to impose on them anything that was merely cultural from his own Asiatic Jewish background.

That, however, brings us to the second area in which the Philippians felt—or said they felt—threatened by the Christian gospel. The laws of the State, they claimed, made it illegal for them as Romans to accept or practise Jewish customs. Now it is understandable that people who live under stern totalitarian governments should be afraid of getting into trouble with the authorities. The last thing they will want to do is to be caught attending some illegal religious meeting. But on this occasion their fears were actually groundless. At this particular period in history (as distinct from what happened twenty or more years later) neither Judaism nor Christianity was banned by the Roman government. And though in theory the Roman government reserved the right to forbid their own citizens from practising foreign religions incompatible with the national religion of Rome, in practice the government did not clamp down on their citizens in this respect.

On the other hand, what was highly illegal—and this the central imperial government did care about enormously—was for a magistrate to flog a Roman citizen publicly and send him to prison without first conducting a thorough and proper investigation. And Paul, the Christian missionary, though a Jew, was also a Roman citizen, the equal of any in Philippi! If the crowd in their fury did not know any better, the magistrates should have known. But this was not the last time that magistrates and judges have acted contrary to their own country's constitution and laws in order to put unwanted Christians behind bars. Yet it makes the Philippians' appeal to the law look less than completely convincing.

Which brings us to the third, and perhaps the strongest, reason why the Philippians felt that the Christian gospel threatened their personal security. Paul's action in putting an end to the medium's ability to tell fortunes cut off one source of supernatural guidance which many people in the city craved for and felt to be an indispensable help to successful living—indeed to survival—in the harsh conditions of the ancient world. And they resented Paul for it, the more so because when he first arrived, the spirit-medium had given him favourable welcome and publicity; but Paul had rejected it and cast the spirit out. For the moment it must have made Christianity appear as an alien, hard-hearted, puritanical, interfering religion that had no feeling for, or sympathy with, the psychological needs of the individual caught up in the frightening complexities of life. No wonder the crowd was furious.

Why then did Paul do it? Precisely because of his compassion and his respect for the sacred inviolability of human personality. The spirit-medium had been invaded and taken over by an alien power. From Luke's description of it as a spirit of Pytho, we gather that when the demon uttered its prophecies through her, the voice that came out of her would not have been her own natural voice, but a strange, unnatural sound. This would have impressed the Philippians as evidence that her prophecies came from some supernatural source. But for Paul, the Christian, it would have produced nothing but compassion for the woman, revulsion at the distortion of a human personality by an evil spirit and sheer indignation that unprincipled businessmen should 'own' a fellow human being and make money out of her distress.

If this was part of the Philippians' culture, then that part was frankly evil. Try to defend it, and on the same ground you would find yourself defending the drug barons and the drug dealers who make money out of destroying people's minds: or the (now banned) practice of suttee in India, where, under pressure from the surrounding culture, a widow feels obliged to sacrifice herself on her husband's funeral pyre.

And then Paul did what he did for the sake of the medium's clients as well. Spiritism, in actual fact, cares nothing for the human personality, but tends to undermine and eventually destroy it. It purports to be able to warn of coming dangers and disasters so that people can then try, if possible, to avoid them. But all in vain; for when accident, disease, and death come, as sooner or later they do, spiritism knows nothing of the love and faithfulness of God the Creator which enables the believer to cry triumphantly, 'I am sure that neither death nor life, nor angels nor rulers, nor things present nor things to come, nor powers, nor height nor depth, nor any thing else in all creation, will be able to separate us from the love of God in Christ Jesus our Lord' (Rom 8:38–39).

This gospel brings a person to know God as loving Father, to experience his salvation, care and guidance. It develops trust in the wisdom of his detailed providences, even when they pass comprehension, reveals the wonder and glory of God's grand and ultimate purposes for his people, and assures them that he will make all the intervening details of life work together for that ultimate good.

Spiritism does nothing at all for the moral development of the human personality; whereas the guidance of the Holy Spirit is predominantly concerned with the development of the person's moral character and increasing holiness.

Spiritism, then, attempts to alter the fundamental conditions which a loving Creator has laid down for human life on earth and so perverts the foundational principles for the development of a secure and mature human personality. It offers foresight of the future instead of present faith in the wisdom, love, and loyalty of the Creator. And without personal faith in God, its Creator and Redeemer, the human personality will ultimately disintegrate, if not in this life then in that which is to come.

Since, then, faith in God through Christ is so absolutely indispensable, it is necessary to distinguish faith both from pagan spiritism or sub-Christian superstition and from genuine spiritual exercise that falls short of what the Christian gospel means by faith. And this, in fact, is the point of one of the last stories which Luke records in this section of his history.

After leaving Europe, Paul eventually spent some time in Ephesus (Acts 19:1-7). There he met twelve men who were disciples of the illustrious prophet, John the Baptist, the forerunner of Jesus. These men were no pagans, therefore; but on their own confession they had never received the Holy Spirit. And why not? Because, while they had learned the necessity of repentance, and doubtless constantly repented of this and that particular sin, they had never learned what it means personally to believe on the Lord Jesus, to believe what he says, to take him at his word, and to enter into a personal relationship with him. Taught by Paul, they, for the first time in their lives, believed on the Lord Jesus and received the Holy Spirit. And to mark the fact that now, and only now, had they become Christians in the true sense of the word, they were baptized in the name of Jesus.

The Holy Spirit, then, as we have said, banishes fear of the future, the haunting fear of failure, the blank dread of death and the grave, the hopeless desolation of bereavement, which are the very things which open people to the dangers of consulting spirit mediums with their amoral guidance, their deceptive comforts and eventual domination of the human personality. The Holy Spirit pours out God's love into the believer's heart and into the depths of his personality (Rom 5:1-11), thus providing a secure basis both for present stability and future moral progress. And that, surely, is no insult to any nation's culture.

CHAPTER 11

Christ among the Philosophers

No civil disturbances followed Paul's preaching of the Christian gospel at Athens, as they had elsewhere. Citizens of the intellectual capital of the world, the Athenians, as Luke points out (Acts 17:16-34), were keen to investigate any new theory that came their way. And so, after some days of general preaching and discussion in the Agora, Paul was invited by Stoic and Epicurean philosophers to address the Court of the Areopagus.

And what did the philosophers think of the Christian gospel? Not much, according to Luke. Before Paul's address, some of them had already dismissed him in contemptuous Athenian slang; and after it, though some were interested to hear more, others openly mocked.

Luke's record at this point, we might think, is at least remarkably honest; but then neither Luke nor Paul would ever have felt tempted to hide the fact that the gospel was foolishness to the Greeks, especially to Greek philosophers. In his writings, Paul advertises the fact that 'Jews demand signs and Greeks seek wisdom, but we preach

Christ crucified, a stumbling-block to Jews and folly to Gentiles' (1 Cor 1:22-23).

This does not mean, of course, that the Christian gospel is anti-rational in the way that, for instance, Zen Buddhism self-confessedly is. Paul urges his converts: 'Be infants in evil, but in your thinking be mature' (1 Cor 14:20). His criticism of human philosophy was not even that it was based on logic rather than faith. Paul knew as well as anybody else that both philosophers and scientists have to accept by faith certain unprovable axioms before they can use logic to erect their systems of thought upon them. Paul's criticism was that, in the nature of things, human philosophy was inadequate for the task of bringing people into a personal living and loving relationship with God: 'the world', he says, 'did not know God through wisdom' (1 Cor 1:21).

The truth of that is evident all around us, and it is no insult to philosophy or to philosophers to point it out. Indeed, the same holds true in other human relationships also. In courtship and marriage, for instance, bare philosophical logic is not normally the means a man uses to win a woman's trust and love, and to induce her to become his wife!

It is not an excess of logic that keeps people from entering into a personal relationship with God, but something much more like ingratitude and pride. All mankind, says the Bible, originally knew God, but 'they did not honour him as God or give thanks to him' (Rom 1:18-21). To be under a constant duty to show gratitude to an almighty Creator is to admit to total dependence on another; and this many people resent and refuse. This is the source of their alienation from God; and the result-ant sin compounds the difficulty: for the guilt it produces makes people instinctively sense God as a threat and an enemy and increases their determination to resist admit-ting to his existence.

To penetrate this barrier of alienation, guilt, fear, enmity, misapprehension and mistrust, God presents not a philoso-phy but a person—and that person is God himself, incarnate in Jesus Christ. He presents not a theory about morality, but a historical event—the cross of Christ, demonstrating, more powerfully than mere words could, the hideous result of man's sin and alienation from God; and simultaneously revealing, as no philosophical argument could, the reality and sincerity of God's love for man in that, while we were still sinners, ungodly, and enemies of God, 'Christ died for us' (Rom 5:5-11). It is by the cross of Christ that man's heart is reached, all barriers between man and God broken down, forgiveness and reconciliation made possible and hope for the future guaranteed.

Now some of the members of the Areopagus Court were Epicureans, some Stoics. Both philosophies were noble attempts to make sense of the universe, its physical workings and man's place within it. Neither was intended to be mere academic theory; both offered practical advice on what man should aim at as his chief goal in life and how to cope with life's pains and sorrows, disasters and evil. But when it came to hope for the elimination of evil from the world, or to any ultimate hope for the individual, neither philosophy had much, if anything, to offer.

Epicureans made pleasure the chief good to be aimed at in life; not the grosser pleasures, for they often involve emotional turbulence, pain and hangover, but pleasure in the sense of trouble-free tranquillity. They therefore advised deliberate withdrawal from too much involvement in the rough and tumble of life. This philosophy in fact produced people who within their own Epicurean fellowships were renowned for their kindness and loyalty; but it was scarcely a philosophy which the ordinary working man, housewife, or business person could practise.

In physics, Epicureans adopted the atomic theory of the earlier philosophers Leucippus and Democritus which they combined with the doctrine of mindless, purposeless, creator-less evolution; and from these theories some of them, like the Roman Lucretius, drew their greatest peace of mind. Those theories proved, they felt, that no part of man survives death; and that therefore all fears of divine judgment and punishment after death are groundless and can be dismissed.

Of course, they did not preach the other side of this Epicurean 'gospel', namely, that if it was true, it meant that the millions of those who in past generations had suffered and died without getting justice in this life would now never get justice; and millions who were currently suffering major or minor injustices had no realistic hope of ever getting justice either. Hope of justice, then, was largely a mirage.

Stoics were very different. They held that at the centre of the universe and pervading all its parts was reason. It was the active agent in creation and controlled all that went on. They referred to this impersonal reason by many names— Nature, Reason, Zeus, God—but this Stoic god was not the transcendent, personal, loving Creator proclaimed by

Judaism and Christianity. He—or rather, it—was as much part of the material substance of the universe as anything else. In other words, the Stoics were pantheists. Unsurprisingly, therefore, when it came to the question of the elimination of evil and injustice from the world, they could offer no more hope than the Epicureans. Since, according to them, reason was at the heart of the universe, pervaded all its parts, ordered and controlled all its happenings, the world-as-it-is was by definition the best of all possible worlds.

Moreover the only real good in life was virtue, defined as living and acting according to reason. All other apparently good things were matters of indifference. So if a wise man saw two million Cambodians about to be massacred by the Khmer Rouge, it would be good and virtuous to attempt to save them. But if, in spite of his efforts, they were massacred, he would not grieve: his effort to save them was rational, therefore absolutely good; the two million lives of themselves were not an absolute good but only a matter of indifference. His own wisdom lay in accepting, without grief or protest, what was now shown to be fate and therefore the outworking of the universal reason.

At first sight, this Stoic teaching might appear the same as the Christian doctrine that 'all things work together for good to those who love God' and that therefore we can and should find comfort in submitting at all times and in all circumstances to the will of God. Actually, it is far removed from it. Christianity does not teach that the world-as-it-is is the best of all possible worlds. The 'good' to which all things work together is not the present world as it is, but the promised 'good' that by divine redemption every believer will eventually be conformed in body and character to the risen, glorified Christ and brought to a world where righteousness reigns.

Stoicism had no such hope. Indeed the earlier Stoics had held that the whole universe, being in its every part and action the expression of universal reason, would at the appropriate time go up in flames and then be renewed exactly the same as it was before. Every event in history would be repeated in precise detail. Evil, then, was forever built into the system. There was only one way out: when circumstances made it impossible for a wise man to live virtuously according to reason, he was allowed to commit suicide!

There is no denying that this philosophy produced many noble, strong, principled characters; but in the end it was a philosophy of hopelessness. And the same is true of the modern equivalents both of the Epicureans (the atheistic evolutionists) and of the Stoics (the pantheists of Hinduism and of the New Age Movement). Paul's comment on the Gentile world at large is especially applicable to both groups: they are not only without God (that is the true God): they are without Christ. They have no sense that God has a deep-laid plan for the redemption of creation and mankind, a plan promised and adumbrated in the Old Testament revelation of his purpose through the nation of Israel, put into action within history by the birth, life, death, resurrection, and ascension of Jesus Christ and scheduled to be brought to its consummation at Christ's second coming. And thus being 'without God' and 'separated from Christ', they are without 'hope . . . in the world' (Eph 2:12).

Of course, there were truths about God that the philosophers of the time could, and sometimes did, perceive by a priori reasoning. Both Stoics and Epicureans would have agreed in principle with Paul's point that the God who made the world and all things in it, should not rightly be thought of as dwelling in temples made with hands (Acts 17:24). It was one of the absurdities of ancient polytheism that the high god, Zeus, had his own special temple in Athens, distinct from the temples of Apollo and of the rest of the gods.

Similarly, the Greek poet, Aratus, himself a Stoic, had written—and Paul quoted it to the Areopagus Court—that we humans are God's offspring (17:28-29). It followed that it was misleading to represent God by dead, impersonal images of wood or metal or stone. We humans are persons; it cannot be that the almighty Power that created us is less personal than we are—though this is the irrational notion which even modern atheism is forced to maintain. And both Stoics and Epicureans would have agreed with Paul that it was self-evident that an almighty Creator who gives to his creatures life, breath, and all things, was not to be served by men's hands as though he needed anything (17:25)—although the notion has persisted from paganism even into some forms of Christendom that we can buy forgiveness and salvation from God by our meritorious deeds. If all the coinage in the world belongs to God by definition, we have no coinage with which to purchase anything from him at all! Like physical life itself, salvation must be a gift.

But what God has done, and will yet do for the redemption of the world, could never be deduced by a priori reasoning from general principles. It is the story of God's sovereign intervention in history; and Paul summed up the basis of the gospel's announcement of a coming sinless world of peace and justice, in these famous words:

> Now [God] commands all people everywhere to repent, because he has fixed a day on which he will judge the world in righteousness by a man whom he has appointed; and of this he has given assurance to all by raising him from the dead. (17:30–31)

At the mention of the resurrection from the dead, Luke tells us, some, though not all, of the philosophers laughed, just as many a scientist today will laugh at the very idea of the existence of God. But they would have done better, as would their modern counterparts, to have thought a little more about the limitations of their philosophical and scientific disciplines. As Prof. Russell Stannard, formerly vice-president of the British Institute of Physics, has written:

> For all its [modern physics'] value as a source of understanding, one has to accept that as an explanatory framework, its scope has its limitations. There are realities, such as consciousness, that lie outside its domain. There are why-type questions . . . that physics is powerless to address . . . it is impossible to take seriously the claim that science has, or will one day have, all the answers. In particular, it is absurd for anyone to assert that 'science has disproved God's existence'. This it could never do.

CHAPTER 12

Christianity and the Right of Free Speech

In the opinion of many, religion is self-evidently a bad thing. It has caused and still causes endless strife and bloodshed and therefore deserves to be rejected. But if that is so, logic would demand the rejection of politics also! For if religion has slain its thousands, politics has slain its ten thousands. However no one seriously argues that political thinking should on that account be abandoned and political activity banned!

The trouble lies, say others, not with religions in general, but with the monotheistic religions, Judaism, Christianity and Islam. Their conviction that their God is the only true God and their religion the only way to him has filled each of them with missionary zeal to force its faith on other people, saving their souls, if need be at the cost of destroying their bodies. Totalitarian ideologies, they admit, stand condemned for the same reason. They, too, have driven people with a similar missionary zeal to export their political systems all round the world and to compel other nations to accept their creed and practice at the cost of untold human suffering. Polytheists, by contrast, so the argument goes, are peacefully prepared to let people believe in any gods they please, and would never dream of forcing their taste in gods on anyone else. Similarly liberal democracies are prepared to let each nation embrace whatever political creed—or religion, for that matter—it pleases without outside interference.

If that be so, Christianity, which is monotheistic and which has been filled with missionary zeal from its birth, has a lot of explaining to do. But that is nothing new. When Luke sat down to write his history of the spread of the Christian gospel, he could not ignore the fact that in many places—Philippi, Thessalonica, Berea, Corinth, Ephesus, Jerusalem—Paul's preaching had been followed by civil unrest, so much so that the matter eventually came to the attention not only of the local magistrates, but of Roman provincial governors, of King Agrippa, and of the Emperor Nero himself.

Of course, it was infinitely easier for Luke to answer for the preaching and behaviour of the Christian apostles and evangelists of the first century AD, than it would be if anyone today tried to defend the plainly indefensible behaviour of which later Christendom has been guilty from time to time. In the first century, Christians obeyed Christ's prohibition on the use of the sword either to promote Christianity or to defend it. Nowhere in the whole of Acts has Luke recorded that the Christians started any of the riots themselves or even retaliated against those who frequently attacked or persecuted them.

Moreover, as the city clerk of Ephesus remarked, the early Christians did not go around desecrating the temples and holy places of other people's religions either (Acts 19:35-37). Though Paul believed, and in his public lectures would have stated, that the pagan gods were not true gods, he did not, according to the same city clerk, denounce pagan gods in abusive and intemperate language calculated to inflame pagan sensitivities.

In Jerusalem, to take another of Luke's examples, the entry of Gentiles into the holy courts of the temple was regarded as a desecration and was strictly forbidden, not only by the Jews but by the Romans, who were anxious to prevent the riots which any breach of this prohibition might provoke. Now Paul, as a Christian, believed that the temple in Jerusalem was fast becoming obsolete. The middle wall of partition (Eph 2:14) that separated Gentiles from Jews in the temple had no place in the Christian gospel. In the Christian churches which Paul founded, believing Jews and Gentiles mixed freely on equal terms without any partition of any kind between them, or between them and God.

In spite of that, when Paul visited the temple in Jerusalem for the last time, he fully respected its rules and regulations, outmoded though they were. He made no attempt to introduce Gentile Christians into the temple or to impose Christian beliefs and practices onto the now antiquated Jewish religious system.

However, Luke explains, he was accused of bringing Gentiles into the temple anyway. This caused a riot and was the reason why he was arrested by the Roman authorities. But the charge was false and never substantiated, as Luke painstakingly makes clear.[1]

In later centuries, admittedly, Christendom behaved very differently. With pagan superstition, and in complete disregard of Christ's prohibition, it sent whole armies on crusades and slaughtered thousands of Turks to recapture the so-called holy places. But to slaughter Christ's enemies is a self-evident and indefensible perversion of the gospel which proclaims that Christ died for his enemies so that they should not perish (Rom 5:10).

Yes, someone will say, but while the early Christians may not have physically assaulted people of other faiths, they did insist on preaching that their God was the only true God, and Jesus Christ the only Saviour, to people to whom they must have known it would be deeply offensive. The Christians therefore are to be blamed for the violent responses which their missionary zeal provoked. Why could they not keep their beliefs to themselves?

This raises far-reaching questions. The early Greek philosopher, Anaxagoras, was put on trial in the Athens of Pericles' day, for teaching that the sun and moon were not gods. Ought he then to have kept silent about the truth so as not to upset the Athenians? Shall we castigate Galileo for proclaiming his belief that the earth goes round the sun, when he must have known the offence and uproar it would cause? Do we not rather admire him?

The right of free-speech is a fragile plant, still often crushed by political and religious tyrannies; for their

1. Acts 21:27–36; 24:1–21; 25:7–8.

power depends on establishing the idea in the minds of the people that their doctrines are the only ones it is safe or legitimate to consider. They must, therefore, prevent the people, if possible, from even hearing minority views.

Moreover, it is a frequently observed human weakness that a movement, while still a minority, will clamour for the right of free speech and protest against its removal; but when that same movement becomes the majority movement, it will in turn seek to suppress all other minority movements.

It happened, alas, with Christendom. The right to evangelize freely, which the apostles and early Christians stood for at such great personal cost and sacrifice, was denied to others by Christendom when it eventually joined forces with the State and became the established religion. It is surely, then, to the credit of true and original Christianity, and not to its shame, that it has always stood with those who have insisted on the universal right and duty to proclaim, with all due courtesy, what one believes to be the truth, and the right peacefully to persuade others of that truth.

There was, of course, one area in which the Christian gospel was easily open to being misrepresented. It proclaimed Jesus as King, or, to put it in Jewish terms, as God's Messiah (= Anointed One). It was easy, therefore, for Christianity's enemies to make out that this was intended in a political sense and was therefore treason against the reigning Caesar.

Luke cites one example (Acts 17:1-9). In Thessalonica the Jews accused the Christians before the local magistrates of 'acting against the decrees of Caesar, saying that there is another king, Jesus' (17:7). The charge was specious, because in Israel itself there were individuals and parties who did interpret the Old Testament promise of a God-sent Messiah in political terms; and from time to time they put up candidates for this role who, they hoped, would drive the hated Roman imperialists out of Palestine by force of arms and restore to Israel their political independence. It was this kind of thing that eventually led to the Jewish revolts of AD 66–70 and 130–33.

Now the early Christian churches believed and preached no such thing. When, in Jesus' lifetime, the crowds had come to make him king by force, Jesus had withdrawn. At his trial before Pilate, the Roman governor, he had made it abundantly clear that his kingdom was not a political, earthly kingdom, to be protected and advanced by force of arms. It was a spiritual kingdom to be propagated by the preaching of God's truth. And when, in spite of this, the Jewish high priests tried to convince Pilate that Jesus was in fact a political activist, both Pilate and Herod gave as their verdict that he was no such thing (Luke 23:1–25).

Similarly when Paul was accused before the Roman courts of subversive political activity, both Gallio, the Roman governor at Corinth, and governor Festus and King Agrippa at Caesarea, after thorough investigation, pronounced Paul completely innocent of any such charge (Acts 18:12–17; 26:31–32).

Luke, for his part, makes clear what Christianity means by proclaiming Jesus as King (17:1–3). The programme which the Old Testament laid down for the promised Messiah, far from stating that the Messiah would set himself up as a political rival to other rulers on earth, prophesied that he would suffer, die, and then be raised from the dead and ascend into heaven. This was the programme which, according to Paul, Jesus had fulfilled. When he comes again to set up his kingdom on earth, it will not be as a merely human politician, vying with other politicians for a share in the government of earth, but as the Lord and Creator of mankind coming with divine right to judge the world and to lead his creation into the next stage of its development.

Unfortunately, Christendom has shown a marked tendency to forget these distinctions and in practice virtually to identify the Christian gospel with this or that political system: in the fourth century with Roman imperialism; in the Middle Ages with feudalism and with absolute monarchy and the divine right of kings; in more recent time with liberal democracy; and still more recently with a Christianized form of Marxism in what is called Liberation Theology. And the prejudice against the Christian gospel which this habit has created in the minds of people and nations who have preferred other legitimate political systems has been regrettable indeed.

There is, then, an urgent need to get back beyond the intervening centuries to the authoritative words of Christ himself:

'My kingdom is not of this world. If my kingdom were of this world, my servants would have been fighting, that I might not be delivered over to the Jews. But my kingdom is not from the world.' Then Pilate said to him, 'So you are a king?' Jesus answered, 'You say that I am a king. For this purpose I was born and for this

purpose I have come into the world—to bear witness
to the truth. Everyone who is of the truth listens to my
voice.' (John 18:36-37)

What then was the truth that Paul proclaimed as he
went around the Roman Empire preaching the kingdom
of God (Acts 20:24-25)? We could perhaps find no better
summary of it than that which Luke has given in recording Paul's appearance before King Agrippa and the Roman
Governor, Festus (Acts 26). After having gone through many
court hearings, Paul was eventually obliged by the intrigues
of his accusers to appeal over the head of the local courts
to the emperor Nero. Partly, then, in order to be able to
send a full report on Paul to the emperor, and partly to sat-
isfy the genuine interest of King Agrippa, Festus arranged
a hearing at which Paul should give an account of himself
and of his beliefs, knowing that what he said might well
reach the emperor's ears and form the basis of his trial. His
speech has become one of the great speeches of history, for,
think what we may of Paul, his influence on the world has
been immense.

He began by recounting his early life and religious
training and then what lay at the heart of his bitter persecution of the early Christians. 'I myself was convinced',
he explained, 'that I ought to do many things in opposing
the name of Jesus of Nazareth' (26:9) Not, we notice, to
oppose Christianity as a religion so much as to oppose
Jesus Christ personally. Jesus was, as far as Paul believed at
the time, dead. But the more he persecuted the Christians
in order to stamp out their beliefs, the more he discovered that it was not a set of religious beliefs that he was

attacking, still less the practice of a system of religious rituals, but the person, Jesus. The Christians claimed that he was alive and that they were somehow in touch with him personally.

To Paul that was utter nonsense; but as the victims of his persecution suffered his tortures, Paul could himself see that it was not just a set of religious beliefs that sustained them but the reality, to them, of the presence of the living Lord Jesus with them. To eradicate Christianity, he would have to eradicate this Jesus. The frustration of it maddened him, goading him to ever more strenuous efforts until the day when the risen Lord met him and spoke to him: 'Saul, Saul, why are you persecuting me? It is hard for you to kick against the goads!' (26:14).

Why had he not seen it before? A superficial answer would be that he had not experienced his supernatural vision of a light above the brightness of the sun before. But then few of his victims, if any, had ever had such a supernatural vision; yet even without it, they had seen with an inner clarity and conviction that brings greater assurance and certainty than even physical eyesight could, that Jesus Christ was alive and available to their personal faith and fellowship.

Why hadn't Paul seen it before? It was not lack of intelligence (he has proved to be one of the master minds of history). It was not lack of religious zeal. What was it, then?

The truth of the matter is, said Paul to Agrippa, that the inner eye of people's hearts is blinded not merely by their own prideful independence of God, self-centredness and sin—though all these things have made their contribution—but by a more than human spiritual power whose evil work it has been to blind men to the reality of God and his love and to inspire in them that same irrational and ultimately Satanic opposition to God that motivates his own wayward spirit (26:18). 'The god of this world [Satan himself]', as Paul wrote elsewhere, 'has blinded the minds of the unbelievers, to keep them from seeing the light of the gospel of the glory of Christ, who is the image of God' (2 Cor 4:4). A man may have perfect physical vision; but if a fog comes between him and the sun, he will not see the sun.

But there is a fog-dispellent, and Paul had seen it work on people a thousand times and more. It was the gospel which the risen Christ commissioned him to preach to the world at large, 'to open their eyes, so that they may turn from darkness to light and from the power of Satan to God, that they may receive forgiveness of sins and a place among those who are sanctified by faith in me' (Acts 26:18).

With powerful confidence Paul urged this gospel on King Agrippa himself. But at that point in the proceedings, Governor Festus bawled across the courtroom, 'Paul, you are out of your mind; your great learning is driving you out of your mind' (26:24). It is extraordinary how irrational some people's reaction to the gospel can be. Before Paul's conversion, he was a persecuting bigot of the bitterest kind. But people did not call him mad for that, any more than people call Stalin mad for sending millions to their deaths because they disagreed with his policies and claimed the right of free speech to say so. But when belief in the gospel turned Paul into a preacher of God's love, who never again persecuted anyone, and whose writings have subsequently brought peace with God to millions, Festus called him mad. If Paul really was insane, perhaps we should pray, God give us more insanity! Or better still, we should turn to Jesus Christ and pray the prayer that myriads of spiritually blind people have successfully prayed: 'Lord, that I may receive my sight.'

For Further Study

If you are interested in examining further the message of the Bible for yourself, the following quotations should be helpful in your study:

> The true light, which gives light to everyone, was coming into the world. He was in the world, and the world was made through him, yet the world did not know him. He came to his own, and his own people did not receive him. But to all who did receive him, who believed in his name, he gave the right to become children of God. (John 1:9-12)

> For God so loved the world, that he gave his only Son, that whoever believes in him should not perish but have eternal life. For God did not send his Son into the world to condemn the world, but in order that the world might be saved through him. Whoever believes in him is not condemned, but whoever does not believe is condemned already, because he has not

believed in the name of the only Son of God. And this is the judgment: the light has come into the world, and people loved the darkness rather than the light because their works were evil. For everyone who does wicked things hates the light and does not come to the light, lest his works should be exposed. But whoever does what is true comes to the light, so that it may be clearly seen that his works have been carried out in God. (John 3:16–21)

For by works of the law no human being will be justified in his sight, since through the law comes knowledge of sin. But now the righteousness of God has been manifested apart from the law, although the Law and the Prophets bear witness to it—the righteousness of God through faith in Jesus Christ for all who believe. For there is no distinction: for all have sinned and fall short of the glory of God, and are justified by his grace as a gift, through the redemption that is in Christ Jesus, whom God put forward as a propitiation by his blood, to be received by faith. This was to show God's righteousness, because in his divine forbearance he had passed over former sins. It was to show his righteousness at the present time, so that he might be just and the justifier of the one who has faith in Jesus. (Rom 3:20–26)

For the wages of sin is death, but the free gift of God is eternal life in Christ Jesus our Lord. (Rom 6:23)

But what does it say? 'The word is near you, in your mouth and in your heart' (that is, the word of faith that we proclaim); because, if you confess with your mouth that Jesus is Lord and believe in your heart that God raised him from the dead, you will be saved. For with the heart one believes and is justified, and with the mouth one confesses and is saved. For the Scripture says, 'Everyone who believes in him will not be put to shame.' For there is no distinction between Jew and Greek; for the same Lord is Lord of all, bestowing his riches on all who call on him. For 'everyone who calls on the name of the Lord will be saved.' (Rom 10:8–13)

For by grace you have been saved through faith. And this is not your own doing; it is the gift of God, not a result of works, so that no one may boast. (Eph 2:8–9)

For they themselves report concerning us the kind of reception we had among you, and how you turned to God from idols to serve the living and true God, and to wait for his Son from heaven, whom he raised from the dead, Jesus who delivers us from the wrath to come. (1 Thess 1:9–10)

Scripture Index

Scripture Index

Other books by David Gooding
(published by Myrtlefield House)

The Riches of Divine Wisdom (NT use of OT)
According to Luke (The Third Gospel)
In the School of Christ (John 13–17)
True to the Faith (Acts of the Apostles)
An Unshakeable Kingdom (Letter to the Hebrews)
How to Teach the Tabernacle
Windows on Paradise (Gospel of Luke)

Other books by John Lennox

God and Stephen Hawking: Whose Design Is It Anyway?
(Lion, 2011)
God's Undertaker: Has Science Buried God? (Lion, 2009)
Gunning for God: A Critique of the New Atheism (Lion, 2011)
Miracles: Is Belief in the Supernatural Irrational?
VeriTalks Vol. 2. (The Veritas Forum, 2013)
Seven Days That Divide the World (Zondervan, 2011)

Myrtlefield Encounters

Myrtlefield Encounters are complementary studies of biblical literature, Christian teaching and apologetics. The books in this series engage the minds of believers and sceptics. They show how God has spoken in the Bible to address the realities of life and its questions, problems, beauty and potential.

Key Bible Concepts explores and clarifies the central terms of the Christian gospel and provides succinct explanations of the basic vocabulary of Christian thought.

The Definition of Christianity throws fresh light on the book of Acts and observes how the first generation of Christians identified and defended the unique features of the gospel.

Christianity: Opium or Truth? offers new perspectives on perennial—and crucial—questions such as the problem of pain and the exclusive claims of Jesus Christ.

The Bible and Ethics presents a concise survey of leading events and people, ideas, poetry, moral values and ethics across both the Old and New Testaments.

About the Authors

David W. Gooding is Professor Emeritus of Old Testament Greek at Queen's University, Belfast and a Member of the Royal Irish Academy. He has taught the Bible internationally and lectured on its relevance to philosophy and world religions. He has published scholarly studies on the Septuagint and Old Testament narratives, as well as expositions of Luke, John 13-17, Acts, Hebrews and the New Testament's Use of the Old Testament.

John C. Lennox, Professor of Mathematics at the University of Oxford, is an internationally renowned speaker on the interface of science, philosophy and religion. He regularly teaches at many academic institutions and teaches the Bible extensively. In addition to his academic works, he has published books exploring the relationship between science and Christianity. He has also participated in a number of televised debates with some of the world's leading atheist thinkers.